TRAMPFACE H
THUMB AND T

By

L.G. West

ISBN: 978-1-9996506-5-0

eBook ISBN: 978-1-9996506-4-3

This is a true story about my time living homeless in the UK whilst hitchhiking. Some names in this book have been changed to protect the individuals involved.

This is my third book in the 'Trampface' Series, following on from the first ground breaking project: Homeless By Choice and the second audacious mission Trampface Calais: Undercover in The Jungle (Migrant Camp). All titles are available on Amazon or from me: Trampface@mail.com

Barrie,

All the best

Dedication

To Mam and all of my friends and family for supporting me through a very difficult year.

Acknowledgements

Rebecca Sparks and 'Ol Angry Red'

Stephen Isaac, my old school friend for the cover artwork.

Sara

Everyone that has supported Trampface, SA1UTE and my project to provide food, support and morale to our frontline workers during the COVID-19 pandemic.

Contents

TRAMPFACE HITCHHIKE

"Thumbing to a Town Near You"

"Who the hell hitchhikes in this day and age?"

"I'll give you until Bridgend before you get bummed and murdered."

"No chance of success. I'll look forward to your seven days of updates from Swansea lads."

"Oh yea, people are going to be queuing up to pick up a 6'4" skinhead and a moody Royal Marine."

It was safe to say that there wasn't much faith in our idea to hitchhike across the country whilst living homeless. The plan was simple, stick our thumbs out by the side of a road going east and wait for some lucky motorist to pick us up. Once inside the vehicle we would use our Trampface charm and ask to be dropped wherever they were going; leaving our adventure totally at the mercy of fate… and the apparent murdering rapists waiting to pick us up, of course.

We could see the flaws and potential for trouble but as Calais had taught us to our benefit: "If you're going to be a Tramp, you may as well be Trampface."

The hitchhike idea was something that I had dreamt about a few years previously, but then it was as a carefree travel adventure rather than a homeless charity challenge. Actually, it was also later on an option in the mix for the social media vote for the first Trampface. I'd always been curious about the exciting and unknown aura surrounding hitching a lift. Putting your trust and hopes in the hands of a complete stranger, the risk of failure and the pure buzz to be felt when a car pulled over; followed by the suspense of waiting to find out where they were going. I think the element of surprise and spontaneity of it would force me to adapt and allow situations that I'd normally avoid. I would be willing to lower my guard in a good way. There's definitely some romance in the notion of drifting wherever the wind (draft of a car) may take you.

Dangerous? Well, yeah no doubt. But if everyone got raped and stabbed when hitchhiking, nobody would ever do it. A few years earlier, I had become a member of an online community called 'Couchsurfing'. The basic premise being that people offer a place for travellers to stay for free; a couch, floor space or even a bed, if you're lucky. You can sign up to 'surf', host or both. When I told most people I was thinking of doing this on an upcoming trip around USA on my leave from Afghanistan, I was met with overwhelming negativity. "Bummed and murdered" were also the buzz words used in this instance. My reply, "Yep, over two million active members and they are all getting raped and murdered." Since that first trip I've hosted and surfed numerous times and met some brilliant people from all around the world; I've hosted groups from Germany, Hungary, Switzerland, Alaska, Austria, France, Italy, South Korea and Canada.

A simple daily activity like catching a bus can be dangerous, plus I've done far more risky things in life than sticking my thumb out for a lift. In fact, I'd already had a small taste of hitchhiking. A couple of years back I had ventured to South America for an eight-week backpacking trip on my own. For some reason I'd got it stuck in my head that it would be fun to hitch a lift to the Welsh town in Patagonia, Puerto Madryn. I'd become adamant at making an attempt, so made a makeshift sign and stood expectantly outside a petrol station. To my delight a local family with Welsh heritage stopped and picked me up. If it was safe in the Badlands of Argentina, then surely 21st century Britain would be Okay.

I decided the best thing to do, to put my mind at ease and prove the doubters wrong was to look it up online. Just to see if there were any statistics or credible sources saying it was completely safe and routine. After all, the sure-fire way to reassure yourself on a subject is to Google it… right?

To nobody's surprise, the most likely results to come up from the search, 'Dangers of hitchhiking' were references to horror movies such as *Texas Chainsaw Massacre* and *The Hitcher*. Popular culture plays along with the cliché of making a hitchhiker appear as a murderous, unhinged, weirdo which feeds into the national psyche of mystique around them. Just like the hitchhiker in *There's Something About Mary*. This then increases the desire for the TV and film producers to exploit fear and elaborate on it. A vicious circle of exaggeration and one that explained the defeatist response we'd received.

I dug a little deeper and found a story about the murder of French hitchhiker Celine Figard near Newbury, UK. An extremely unpleasant story which didn't dissuade my plans but did give me food for thought. That tragic incident was back in 1995, so surely an isolated event. I now had a taste for research on the topic and the first comment we'd received about our plan echoed in my mind, "Who the hell hitchhikes in this day and age?" I wondered if anyone still did.

Hitchhiking has been in heavy decline since the 70s. Anyone that has driven, or paid attention whilst a passenger in a car, over the last couple of decades will have noticed that. They will have also noticed that there are indeed some hardy souls still out there doing it. I've passed many over the years, mostly hippie-type looking males with large backpacks. I'd never been averse to it but always found that by the time I spotted them, I was either going too fast or didn't make the decision quickly enough to stop. I've only once ever picked one up and I was a little disappointed by the encounter…

I'd been driving back from an exercise in Herefordshire along the 'Heads of the Valleys' road in South Wales. I'd approached a large, open roundabout that had a view across it from my direction of travel. I could see a man in a colourful waterproof jacket on the grass verge of my exit. He had a sign saying 'Swansea' and looked to be in his forties, tubby and relatively harmless. He'd picked his spot well as 30 metres past his chosen spot was an easily identifiable layby. I pulled over and he approached my car and hopped in. He put his cardboard sign away amongst a pile of other prewritten ones and it soon became clear why he had happened to be in such a good spot. He was a professional.

He made a living picking up cars from dealerships, hire companies and repair shops. Instead of them sending two employees in a car to pick one up for them to then drive both vehicles back, they pay this man to bring it one way. Their conditions being that he finds his own way there. To save himself money he hitchhikes to the nominated city, picks up the car and drives it home or sometimes to another city and then hitchhikes home. He told me that sometimes he doesn't go home for days but just bounces around hitching and delivering cars. I was sceptical about his success rate and asked if he spends a lot of time waiting around or resigns to paying for transport at times. He enthusiastically replied, "Not at all, I never find myself waiting long before a pick up. I was only there for five minutes before you came along." I was surprised by this but it made sense if he was earning a living from it.

The hitchhiker asked to be dropped at a Skoda garage just outside Swansea. I had no prior engagement so had no problem dropping him to the door. He thanked me and I wished him well as he jumped out. It wasn't the *conversation* that I was disappointed with, it had been really interesting and informative and the man was friendly and engaging. It was just that I'd much preferred to have picked up what I perceived a regular hitchhiker to be; someone carefree and on an adventure with tales of triumphs and mishaps along the way. I'd wanted someone in a less business-like situation. Maybe I'd been the one believing too many clichés in movies.

I decided to wind down my research with some good old fact finding and a search for statistics. The problem was that a lot of it was based on opinion and estimation. A German study concluded that the actual risk is much lower than the public perceived it to be and it did not advise against hitchhiking in general. They suggested that in some cases there were verbal disputes or inappropriate comments but physical attacks were very rare.

The problem was that limited data is available regarding the safety of hitchhiking. Compiling good safety data requires counting hitchhikers, counting rides and crucially – counting problems; a difficult task as I guess it's hard to report a problem to the 'Hitchhiker Safety Executive' when you're buried in a ditch (after a good bumming)!

WEDDING BELLS, TRAMP 2 SMELLS

"The Lady Needs Her Tramp"

"Westy, I need your bloody help!"

I was sat in my room on my base in South Devon when this cry for help came from the other end of my phone. Ceri, Tramp 2's girlfriend, wasn't normally someone that would routinely ring me for a chat so I knew something was urgent. I told Ceri I was there for her and nervously asked her to continue.

"It's Paul, he's going to book a skiing holiday for a week, leaving this Saturday. He's going to take James and Darcy (his sons) to the Alps." I was relieved that it didn't actually seem like a serious problem and was about to tentatively question what the issue was when Ceri continued. "It's Valentine's Day on Sunday." I now rolled my eyes from the safety of the other side of the phone in Devon and was still not convinced there was a problem I could help with. I think Ceri could sense my lack of enthusiasm and she knew only too well how unromantic and unsensitive I was regarding these occasions. She proceeded to download a full explanation:

"A couple of months back I entered a competition on the Wave (local radio station). It was asking for suggestions about how a woman could propose to her partner in an unorthodox way; this year is a leap year, the traditional time for the roles to be reversed. They were looking for quirky and interesting ideas of how girls would do it and the best three would be chosen to go into the final. From there the radio station would set up for all three girls to go through with their proposals in front of a film camera. The listeners then get to watch the link and vote on who should win. The winning couple will receive an arranged and paid for wedding at a plush venue worth £20,000. I've been selected, we are in the final!"

I was stunned by Ceri's story but happy for her, "Whoa, that's awesome Cer, well done mush," I replied. But then the way she had finished the story made me curious… "What do you mean *we* are in the final?" Ceri giggled and said, "Well, let me explain again."

"My proposal involves Trampface. The plan was that Badge and Claire, the presenters, would get in touch with you two boneheads and say that they'd heard about the fantastic event you do for charity each year. They would woo you with wanting to hear about the adventures and invite you into the studio to chat on air. Knowing that you two mouthy, show offs would love the chance to tell stories live on the radio it would be a sure thing. Once you two were half way through the interview we'd have a break… and then I would appear and propose to him live in the studio."

I couldn't help but laugh and replied, "Fair play that is brilliant."

Ceri agreed and continued, "The problem now is that the interview is set for this Sunday, Valentine's Day. But he's going to book that bloody skiing holiday when he gets home tonight. It's going to ruin everything Westy, you are going to have to do something and stop him somehow. It was meant to be a surprise to you both but I had to ring you because I can't see any other way of stopping him or sorting it out. I'm a nervous wreck."

We both calmed down and spent some time hatching a plan. The direction we would take would be for me to speak to him and break the news that the Wave had contacted me and wanted to do a full live interview on Sunday. I'd attempt to play an angle on two things that I knew would get me leverage; Tramp 2's love of Trampface and his pleasure in talking about it in the limelight. One difficulty we faced was trying not to spook him into thinking something was off. If I was too forceful or out of character he would latch on to it. He's a switched-on bloke and would know if I was acting unnaturally. I was now in on the plan and fully wanted it to work out; how could I resist the chance to completely stitch up my best mate live on radio!

I waited a few hours and then spoke to Paul:
"Alright my boy, I've got some exciting news… Badge and Claire from the Wave want to interview us about Trampface. Awesome or what?"
"Serious? Wow that's awesome my boy. When do they want the Tramps?"
"Sunday morning."
"This Sunday? I can't make it as I'm about to book skiing with James and Darcy. Can't we reschedule?"
"Afraid not my boy, they said it has to be this Sunday as they are doing a charity special and picking local causes to promote. It's a one day offer only as we will be kicking it off. Headliners as such."
"Nightmare. This deal I've found is gleaming and it's not often I can take the boys skiing, especially at affordable prices."
"Come on my boy, you can go skiing another time. How many chances do we get with this kind of media exposure? With Hitchhike coming up it would give us a right boost."
"Yea I know my boy. Let me have a look at dates and think about it. I'll ring you later."
"Sweet my boy, give my love to Ceri… haven't spoken to her in ages."

Tramp 2 seemed to have taken the bait. We both knew each other inside out by now, so I had an easy time gauging his reaction and feelings. I hoped that didn't work against me and lead to him being suspicious. After my exchange with Paul I waited an hour or so and rang Ceri for an update. She had told him that the reason she didn't want him to go skiing was that she had planned a special Valentine's day and night out and paid for it.

"He's going mad at me, saying I'm ruining his chances of taking the boys skiing. He's asked me what is so special about my plan that we can't just do it another weekend. I've told him I can't tell him as it would ruin the surprise but that I've paid and can't get a refund. I feel awful Westy, like he thinks I'm selfish and purposely trying to derail his trip with the boys."

We decided that I wouldn't push it any further as it would seem too much like a coordinated attempt at stopping him going skiing and thus draw suspicion. We agreed that we had both given our best pitch and it was now down to him to decide what he wanted. We hoped that his kind nature and loyalty towards us would swing the balance in our favour. It was a nervy few hours and at around 11pm we had our answer. Tramp 2 text me, "I'm in my boy, what time do they want us Sunday?"

GET ME TO THE ALTAR

"Riding the Wave"

Ceri and Paul live next to the beach in Aberafan, a district of Port Talbot. It is a beautiful stretch of coast just seven miles across the bay from Swansea. It is sometimes overpowered by the sight and smell of the massive steelworks which is one of the biggest in the world and employs an estimated 10% of the town's population. The name 'Port Talbot' first appears around 1837 after the building of a new dock near the River Afan by the well-known Talbot family. Early evidence of humans in the area dates back to the Bronze Age with farming ditches as old as 4000 BC. Iron Age hill forts have also been excavated and the famous deer herd of Margam were first introduced by the Roman Conquerors.

Port Talbot's rise to prominence was attributed to the industrialisation of the area, notably from the establishment of a copper works in 1770. The River Afan was diverted to accommodate the transport of copper and raw materials.

Despite possessing a modest population of approximately 38,000 the town boasts a proud and impressive list of notable 'sons': **Richard Burton**, the notorious actor who starred in a glittering array of feature films between the 1950s and his death in the early 1980s. He was also famous for his marriage to Elizabeth Taylor and his alcoholism that during its peak saw him drinking three bottles of vodka a day. **Sir Anthony Hopkins**, probably best known for his portrayal of Hannibal Lecter in *The Silence of the Lambs.* More recently he has starred in the Marvel *Thor* films. **Michael Sheen OBE**, actor in *Frost/Nixon, The Damned United, Tron: Legacy and Twilight: New Moon.* **Rob Brydon**, Welsh actor and comedian. **Paul Potts**, winner of *Britain's Got Talent* and opera singer. Finally, most amusing of all, **Captain Beany**, a bloke who paints himself to look like a giant bean and raises money for charity. He has set a world record for the longest time spent in a bath of baked beans and had 60 beans tattooed on his head. The people that sponsored him were granted their inked initials on one of the beans.

Paul and Ceri met on the hiking expeditions that he organised through the gym he owned. I would join him on these trips as an extra safety guide for tackling peaks like Snowdon and Ben Nevis, which had very temperamental weather systems liable to changing quickly, and dangerously. A lot of the walkers would be fairly inexperienced in arduous treks in such difficult conditions, so we would ensure they were correctly prepared and that we carried safety equipment. The trips were always enjoyable as the group were a great laugh and enjoyed our sense of humour… and well, if not, they were able to put up with ours at least! Trips would inevitably revolve around a social night and drinks and over time Ceri and Paul became close.

On one particular trip up Snowdon, another famous resident of Port Talbot tagged along. His screen and local nickname is Pancho, and he was the star of a show called *Dirty Sanchez*; a kind of Welsh *Jackass* but far more brutal, funny and extreme. During that particular trip he spent the whole slog up to the peak swigging cans of Strongbow cider, the same drink we had dabbled with on Trampface Swansea. Pancho was always the focal point of practical jokes on the show, usually resulting from him falling asleep or just being crazy and careless. This was absolutely not a show for the cameras and he was a larger than life lunatic and party animal in real life also. I had a very surreal and comical moment with him once whilst sharing a couple of beers. He had been chatting normally when he suddenly stopped and said to Paul and me, "Fair play, that thing you did in Calais with the migrants was absolutely mental. You two are off 'ew heads mun."

There we were, two pretty normal blokes, being told by one of the craziest people on TV that we were off our heads for doing Trampface. Truly a moment to treasure and laugh about.

The Friday before our date with Badge and Claire, I had been in London for a 30th birthday bash. It was with two Brazilian friends, Danni and Lucy, that I had met through the community I previously mentioned: Couchsurfing. We'd originally met in Brighton where a host and some German 'surfers' I had hosted in Swansea were having a party. I was on a shooting exercise in Kent (same location as when I had done my reconnaissance trip to Calais) and had been invited. We'd remained friends and stayed in touch and on this occasion I was paying them a visit in London.

My train journey home on Saturday was a little subdued but I was buzzing at the thought of the interview the next day and surprising Tramp 2. I couldn't help but laugh thinking about how he would react. Ceri and Paul were a perfect match for each other and basically married without the legal status. They had no plans for immediate marriage because they had already made a commitment which they were happy with and a wedding is very expensive. In my eyes it's just a formality and a good old day out and party. He surely wouldn't see this coming but I was still worried that he'd somehow worked it out and was going to turn it around on us. Ceri was a little worried as the station had been promoting it non-stop and he listened to the show in work.

My house is between the radio station and Paul's house in Port Talbot so the plan was for him to pick me up en route. It had only been a couple of days since Ceri and I had hatched our plan and I hadn't seen Tramp 2 in the meantime. I hopped into Paul's van and braced myself for a face to face grilling about the interview. No doubt he would want to probe a little and not giving away any 'tells' was easy on the phone, not so easy though when sat next to your best friend of a couple of decades.

The questions started immediately, "So how did they find out about Trampface and manage to contact you?" He'd gone straight in for the kill.

"Ummm, they said someone had told them about it and they followed it up with a search of our page."
"Cool. So what is this charity event, I've not heard anything on the Wave this week about it?"
"Yea, they are doing all the interviews and preparation work today so they can then tailor the promotion to exactly what they've got from Monday."
"So we are not live then?"
"Yea, we are live as an impromptu broadcast for the listeners and then the radio will say that in light of our great story they are going to run an extended promotion throughout the week. Awesome or what?"
"Yea fair play my boy, awesome."

I'd bluffed him; the rest of the journey was spent cracking jokes about what we shouldn't say on the radio and the angle that we *should* approach with. I'd spent so much time concentrating on keeping to my story about the interview, I had spent hardly any time thinking about my actual performance. It didn't really pose a problem though, we were approaching our third Trampface and had spent many hours explaining our mission to people. We knew the interesting parts off by heart and had long worked out how to sum it up in intriguing and short pitches.

The radio station was in a small building just off a busy road on the outskirts of Swansea. We pulled into the car park and headed straight into the reception. Ceri and her sister Beth were hiding around the corner; they had told Paul they were going shopping that morning to enable Ceri to meet up with the promotion staff. Once inside we introduced ourselves and were offered a drink and a seat. Faye, the girl I had spoken to on the phone entered and wasted no time in making excuses for being out drinking until the early hours! This made her fair game for some Trampface ribbing and we all participated in some light banter. Faye was joined by Alice and they both made small talk whilst we waited to be briefed for our interview. Faye's still tipsy state nearly blew the whole thing when she asked Tramp 2, "So how often do you go skiing?" A fairly innocuous question but I could see the look of curiosity on his face. Faye clearly knew about the close call with the skiing booking and was just thinking on the hoof about possible chit-chat. I could sense the tension and said to Paul, "I told them we couldn't confirm until you'd made a decision about skiing."

Faye and Alice were both young attractive girls and we chatted easily with them. They were both attached and were asking questions about Valentine's Day plans. I giggled when Paul said, "Umm yea, the missus has booked something, it's a surprise though."

I found it fascinating walking through the studio of a radio station I had listened to since a young age. I'd always pictured what it would look like and of course I'd imagined it to be like a Hollywood studio. It was modern with clean edges but a little cramped. We walked down a thin corridor with picture frames of famous musicians and soon came to a stop near a serious looking door with an 'On Air' light outside. This was it, Trampface was going live and Tramp 2 was either getting engaged or slapped in the face and abused by every woman in South Wales!

We settled into our executive black chairs with big microphones in front of us and made nervous small talk with the host 'Badge'. He looked different to the radio world of characters I'd pictured in my head. I'd imagined him to be a short, chuckling, cheesy presenter in the '80s mould but he was tall, healthy and really easy to talk to. It wasn't long before the call came to go live. It was interesting to hear the song being played live on the radio in low volume knowing that when it ended our voices would be broadcasting across the soundwaves.

The mics went live and everything went better than we expected. Badge was enthusiastic and positive and we managed to get across some key points about the Trampface mission. I enjoyed it. The intermission came and I suddenly became aware of what was going to happen. Just before going live again an entourage started creeping into the studio, one by one, including a cameraman. Tramp 2 gave me a curious sideways look and he got a shrug back from me. I then acted on my prior instructions and stood up from my chair (strategically placed closest to the door) and moved to stand by the opposite wall. Tramp 2 now shot me a look of absolute bewilderment at my actions and started looking around, wondering why his wingman had stood up and walked off. His search for an explanation didn't last long.

I was expecting Ceri to walk in like her brash, confident, kick-ass self and pin Tramp 2 to the soundboard before demanding his hand in marriage. She wasn't quite that forceful and the pure emotion and desire of the occasion had clearly got to her. She walked in, sat down next to him and delivered the most heartfelt proposal ever, through genuinely uncontrollable tears, ending with:

"This lady needs her Tramp."

If you watch the video back you may see/hear a certain other Tramp present wipe a tear and exclaim, "Has someone been cutting onions in here?"

He said, "Yes", thankfully. He was in complete shock, that was certain. He definitely didn't look like he had seen it coming. The exit was a bit of a blur. We had to leave and they had a radio show to get on with. Ceri and Beth told us to meet them at a local pub to have a bottle of champagne to celebrate so we headed back to the van. Once inside, Paul let out a massive lungful of air and brushed his hand over his head. He turned to me and said in a shell-shocked manner, "Did *you* know that was going to happen?" I burst out laughing and said, "Of course I did you header, done you like a kipper my boy."

Tramp 2 gave me some stick about stitching him up live on air and I asked him if he honestly had any idea something was up. "Not at all my boy, didn't have a clue and wasn't expecting that at all." The surprise had worked and as Tramp 2 sat looking out the window in a daze I asked him what he thought about it now the dust was settling. "I've only just recovered from my first fucking marriage." We spent another couple of minutes laughing and it got even worse when Tramp 2 said, "Imagine if I'd said I didn't have a missus to Faye and Alice in the reception and we'd tried to flirt with them... minutes before they were leading me in to get proposed to."

The proposal was done and the two other competing couples had also completed theirs. The others were also good ideas, one was on the pitch at half-time during a Swansea City football match but it was really painful to watch. The girl just blurted it out without any emotion and the guy had to be prompted to answer by the poor presenter who was battling through it. The other proposal was just before a movie screening at the local cinema. I am clearly biased but even trying to look at it objectively I knew that we had the strongest one. You may notice I said "we". Well yes, even though it was their proposal and marriage I felt like it was a team event. We were all in it together and I suppose the Trampface element made me feel more invested also.

Next up we faced something that played right into our hands... begging! The Wave had posted all of the proposals online and challenged the listeners to watch and vote for their favourite. Despite my confidence that our proposal was the strongest by far, it was down to a straight-out fight for votes and in the lap of the networking gods. We set straight to task getting everyone we knew to go online and vote. Paul is a bit of a well-known celeb in Port Talbot so we would get a good head start. I was in the middle of instructing a promotion course so had a captive audience of 60 Royal Marines in a classroom that I could order to get their phones out! The day of the result approached and we waited on tenterhooks.

The result was broadcast live on the radio and the sound of Ceri's beaming voice was confirmation that we'd won. Tramp 2 text me and said, "Looks like you've got a speech to write my boy." I'd hoped that he'd pick me as his best man and I guess many people would've thought it was just a formality. But we had only met when we were 20 years old and he had many childhood friends. I would therefore be best man with one of them, Tomo, who was also now a good friend of mine. I felt honoured. The wedding was to be sited in the plush surroundings of Oldwalls on the Gower Peninsula. The date was April, just two months away, meaning time was of the essence in order to prepare for it… lots to be done in a short space of time and it didn't help that the groom and best man were disappearing for a week of hobo hitchhiking two weeks prior to the big day.

"If we end up somewhere decent maybe we can coordinate it with a stag do my boy."

ON YOUR MARKS

"Here Thumb the Tramps"

The lead up to our third annual Trampface mission was a little different to the previous ones. In the past I had felt subdued and anxious during the countdown and pondered on my reasons for doing it and potential outcomes. This one felt like a good old-fashioned carefree adventure. It felt like it was going to be extremely enjoyable and light-hearted and we were eager to get going. The only real concern we had was not getting any good stories, but we had thought that on the other missions and they turned out better than we could've imagined. The fact was, that no matter what we did when together, stories always followed. I was positive that Hitchhike would be the same.

The preceding days of T-Day took on a familiar pattern; drunken meetings laughing about previous stories and possible new encounters. As ever we needed a few things sorted before setting off: a charity page, a set of rules and guidelines to follow and a good cover story, of course. "Right then my boy, let's get this cover story sorted."

"Once picked up we'll give it ten minutes of awkward silence and then say that we are fugitives from the law. Wanted for violent murder."
"Escaped mental patients, looking to get back to Stonehenge for a pick up via spaceship."
"Freedom fighters heading to Syria to fight against ISIS… or even better converted Muslims going to join and fight *for ISIS."*
"Mormon missionaries, travelling the land spreading the message of our Lord. Ask if we can put the Bible FM station on the radio"
"Male prostitutes, heading to London to make it big."

We settled on a less fanciful and more believable cover story: Two council house evictees now destitute and hitching to London to find work on the building sites.

Our charity of choice would once again be SSAFA. The rules would follow a similar theme to Trampface Swansea and were posted online for everyone to see:

Tomorrow is T-Day... we will once again be giving up a week of our personal annual leave to go homeless without support for the military charity SSAFA!
If you'd like to share and support our page of updates can I ask you to please write a few words to explain and encourage people to support and donate! Or use our blurb! So this is the plan...

Trampface HitchHike Rules:
We will start in Swansea 18th March with a sign saying "Going East/Anywhere" and attempt to thumb a lift.
Once we are picked up we will proceed to the same location as the driver (or where ever they kick us out) and spend a night homeless sleeping rough.
The next day we will again attempt to thumb a lift to 'anywhere' and continue the process of sleeping rough and hitching each day.
We are not permitted to use any of our own money or accept favours from friends and can only rely on begging in order to provide money or food/water.
Whilst begging we will NOT tell people about Trampface, we will pose as ex-forces who are on the streets until we can sort ourselves out (like TF Swansea). Also travelling to London looking for work. This will provide a real experience of living rough. If we are challenged by the authorities or end up in a situation of no choice we will quietly explain our project.
Whilst hitchhiking we are permitted to tell the occupants of the car our mission, reasons being we have already been picked up and we have nothing more to gain by lying to them. We can then gauge their opinion and trade stories... we may however use our cover story on the odd driver just for a laugh.
Unlike TF Swansea we may decide to accept a night of temporary homeless housing if offered. This would provide a new angle and

experience of the process, how we are treated and how we are accepted by the well-known homeless in the area... especially with our accents!
We are permitted to do anything a homeless person would otherwise be able to do. This is our overriding condition.
We will carry phones. Despite the fact that most homeless people we met last time also have them, they provide the means to document the project via pictures and daily updates.
We are permitted one item of warm covering, thin sheet or fleece etc... which will consist of something of a size no bigger than a double pack of kitchen roll.
Towards the end of the 7 days we will make an assessment on how far away we are and whether we will have to pay for public transport home. We will choose whatever is best for the story and experience.
We will document any money we spend on food from the begging money and pay that back from our own money after the 7 days, along with any other begging money gained (if any) which will be paid into the charity fund.
We will carry our passports... who knows, someone may be going through Calais. Jungle part 2?

Text HOBO88 to 70070
Lots of thumbing love...
Hiker 1 and Hiker 2

Our final decision was on our clothing. Paul had some old desert fatigues and a scruffy, thin, black jacket. I had some old grey trousers and the same jacket from the first two Trampface missions. If it's not broke, don't fix it. We both had red hoodies underneath our jackets. We had a pretty convincing look which had been honed from past missions and we knew that after a day of 'sleeping' rough we'd soon look like the cast of *Dad's Army* fallen on hard times.

I'd finished work in Devon on the Thursday and driven home to Swansea that night, in readiness for an early start. The plan was to meet for breakfast just off to the side of the main expressway out of Swansea. I was excited about the adventure and couldn't wait to see who picked us up… if anyone actually did.

TRAMPFACE HITCHHIKE T-DAY

"A False Start is Still a Start"

Swansea (Abertawe in Welsh) is a coastal city in South Wales with a population of 240,000. It's more of a large town really and if you go any further west you will only encounter smaller rural towns and areas; no good for some busy Trampface action. The town centre is fairly dilapidated and mundane due to a rapid building scheme after it was unexpectedly blitzed by the Luftwaffe during the Second World War. Notable people include **Dylan Thomas**, the legendary boozy poet and writer who a certain Tramp may emulate and aspire to (do not at all take that as me comparing myself to his writing ability but more his habits whilst doing it) and **Catherine Zeta Jones**, the very exotic looking film actress and proud Swansea girl. During my world travels I'm always forced to get Google out to prove to foreigners, who think she is from Latin America, that they are wrong. That's probably it on the notable people front apart from the football team with its admirable run of Premier League status.

Some things that you probably didn't know about my hometown:
In 2004 Swansea was named Britain's wettest city (we could attest to that after Trampface Swansea).
It was once nicknamed 'Copperopolis' due to the huge volume of copper manufactured in the city and was at one point the largest exporter of copper in the world; until the USA slapped restrictions on foreign imports to develop its own industry.
People from Swansea are called and refer to themselves as 'Jacks'. This is due to the rich maritime history of the 'Coppermen' from Swansea dominating the waves. 'Jack' is slang for sailor. It was once said that if you turned up at any port in the world and introduced yourself as a Swansea Jack, you would immediately be taken on as a ship hand; such was the reputation, skill and experience of the Cape Horners (another nickname from their regular and successful trips around the treacherous Cape Horn). The 'Jack' nickname is also connected to Swansea's most loved citizen… a dog that became a lifeguard and saved 27 people (and

one dog) from drowning in the bay during the seven years of his life (1930–1937). Our beloved and heroic dog has a monument dedicated to him, overlooking Swansea Bay where he carried out his selfless acts of lifesaving.

It was apparently first named 'Swein's ey (Island)'. Legend has it that Swein was a Norseman that built a fort in Swansea in 100AD to conduct raids into West Wales. The modern fountain in the City centre sits in front of a contrasting backdrop; the decaying ruins of a Norman castle built in 1107 (timber and partly destroyed by Welsh rebel forces) and fortified in stone in 1221. It once survived a 10-day siege with the residents close to absolute starvation. If you stand on the fountain side today you can line up the remaining tower of the castle with the modern, glass windowed BT office tower behind; it gives a striking view with the modern tower lined up in perfect symmetry and appearing to grow out from the top of the castle.

I think the most amazing fact about the area is that the world's first ever discovery of a human fossil was in the County of Swansea (Gower Peninsula). The Red Lady of Paviland was found in a cave on the ragged shoreline covered in red ochre and surrounded by 'jewels' and items of tribute. It was named so in the belief that it was a female due to its size, however, it turned out to be a small male. Dating proved it to be 34,000 years old and remains to this day, the oldest ceremonial burial of a human in Western Europe. At the time of his life, the cave would have been over 70 miles inland. The fossils of our Red Lady now sit in a museum in Oxford and the cave is on private restricted land. It is only accessible by the hardiest souls, by either abseiling down or accessing via the sea and a climb at low tide.

Back to present day Swansea and there was soon to be a couple of modern fossils, red in the face and meeting a different kind of copper. The sun was shining bright at 8am this Friday morning and the Tramps were sat in good spirits in a café enjoying a coffee. Tramp 2 asked if I'd brought the hitching sign and I replied, "Yea, sort of. I've got the cardboard and a black marker. I thought it would be fitting to actually make it while deployed over the start line. Doing it for real innit?" Tramp 2 sniggered and said, "Go on then get a move on."

I was head down with tongue out doing my best to concentrate on making the sign legible and noticeable to a speeding car and oblivious to my surroundings. Tramp 2 said, "Coppers my boy." I mumbled something back and he nudged me in time for me to see two policemen in motorbike uniforms looking over my shoulder. I shuffled the sign away and they laughed. Tramp 2 shook his head and I said, "Don't worry, hitchhiking isn't illegal. I looked it up and the only thing illegal is if you are doing it on a road that doesn't permit pedestrians, like a motorway etc. That's why you see most of them on slips roads and A roads." The cops sat down and I finished the rest of my masterpiece.

Our first spot to kick off the mission was just across the road and the initial signs seemed promising; loads of traffic. Fabian Way is a major arterial route in and out of Swansea. We hoped that with it being a Friday, there would be lots of people heading east for the weekend. Our spot was strategically placed just before a set of traffic lights and near the entrance to a petrol garage; allowing motorists to slow for the lights and identify a place to pull in. We felt very unsure and tentative about our chances of a pickup but were optimistic about a story either way. Not long after we had stood facing the oncoming traffic with our sign a familiar face passed by. Vicky, who had promised us a stapler whilst we were begging during Trampface Swansea, gave us a beep and a wave but still no stapler; Admiral must be suffering from stationery cutbacks.

Ten minutes passed with Tramp 2 holding the sign for his allotted time in our 'shift' pattern. There were some curious looks but mostly we were getting ignored. In my mind I had settled for a good hour or so of waiting around. Paul stood firm and was confident our luck would be in, rightly so when he excitedly called out to me,

"2003 silver Ford approaching and slowing down with the driver looking at us my boy." The car screeched to a sideways halt in the garage entrance and then reversed towards us. Jackpot. The driver was waving at us so we hurried over towards him.

Tramp 2 leaned into the wound down passenger window and bold as brass said, "Where are we going drives?" The driver replied, "You tell me lads?" and we piled in. Heading east we quickly started chatting with the driver who introduced himself as Steve, a former Royal Navy Engineer Officer. He had been in Swansea temporarily conducting software training for the power plant. After he'd explained his background we told him about the Trampface mission and our own back stories. We relayed our wish to get to as many far away and different places as possible and then asked him where his final destination was… "North Yorkshire lads."

Wow. We had hit the best start we could have ever imagined, aside from someone going abroad. Within ten minutes by the side of the road we had been picked up by a friendly bloke travelling 300 miles to a different country and area where we would really stick out. Steve had a South East Asian look to him and looked and talked very much like an educated and business-like man. He was however, dressed like a chav, with comfortable tracksuit bottoms, trainers and cap. Fair enough for a five-hour drive north I suppose.

After around 20 minutes of driving and chatting, Steve had mentioned a red light flickering on his display. We ignored him and Tramp 2, sat in the front because he's lanky, launched into the full history of Trampface. A further ten minutes passed of tales and we realised that the earlier red-light warning had actually been more important than our stories. Steve turned to Tramp 2 and said, "We're gonna have to stop lads." Tramp 2 responded in typical playful fashion and said, "Why mush, bored of my stories already are ew?"

With a clunk of metal inside Steve's bonnet and a swerve of his steering wheel, we saw the green grass bank of the hard shoulder rapidly approach us. "Shit," we all yelled and luckily Steve managed to guide the car to a stop on the tarmac. Just minutes earlier, we had been ecstatic with being on our way to the North of England and a mighty start to the week, but we now found ourselves stranded ten miles from Cardiff.

Our spirits had been lofty after our pickup, but the only thing *up* now was the bonnet of Steve's car. Our moods were like this once majestic silver car – broken down. Trying to find a solution I quizzed Steve whilst he was tinkering with the engine like most blokes would do in this situation… basically he had no idea what the problem was but had to look like he did. We've all been there! "So, Steve, what breakdown cover have you got?" I asked, confidently. I was certain a former officer of Her Majesty and now diligent lecturer would be covered for breakdown. Steve bowed his capped head in the manner of being slightly embarrassed and then looked sideways at me and said… well he didn't actually say anything, he just let out a nervous laugh and shook his head whilst smiling apologetically.

I turned to Tramp 2 and burst out laughing. Yes, it was a nightmare considering we had thought we were on our way north and now found ourselves sat on a motorway embankment. But it was brilliant for Trampface, we were previously worried about getting stories and here we were 30 minutes after the first pickup, broken down miles from anywhere. I smiled at Tramp 2 and he said, "You couldn't write it my boy."

Luckily for Steve, I had AA breakdown cover with my bank account benefits, which allows recovery for any vehicle I am travelling in. Probably a little bit outside of the Trampface rules but the right thing to do I'm sure you'd agree. The situation had been turned on its head from Steve doing us a good turn to us being his saviour. Being 250 miles from home with a broken car and no cover would have turned out to be more expensive than Steve's old car was worth.

We were ready to sit it out for a time again, but much like our first pickup the next one arrived much sooner than we'd anticipated. A mere 20 minutes later, Steve's shed was on the back of a flatbed and we were inside the cab torturing the driver, John, with stories. John gave Steve two options, he could tow him all the way home, although it would entail swapping over to different agents at certain area borders. Or he could pull into the services and we could wait while he purchased the parts needed and returned to fix the car on the spot.

Steve treated us to croissants and coffee (not strictly allowed in the rules we know but it seemed fair) at the services while poor old John cracked on changing the alternator outside. Steve really was a great bloke and we had a pleasant half an hour chatting about military stories and his life now. He told us that he couldn't follow us online as he had no social media or Internet presence whatsoever. Totally off the grid digitally. Tramp 2 pointed out that it was a bit ironic considering he was a software engineer. Although his knowledge of his field may have been the specific reason why he was off grid. Steve asked what our intentions were, as we had been deliberating over whether to continue north with him or not. We decided that since time was getting on and we would hit serious Friday traffic on the way north, resulting in a very late arrival, we'd change tact. We agreed the mission would be much better served if he would kindly drop us in Cardiff so that we could make the most of the day begging and interacting. Plus, there was an international rugby match being played the next day and *that* would surely provide a great opportunity to experience begging amongst a drunken crowd.

En route to Cardiff we joked about the sequence of events and said how impressed we were with the efficiency of the AA. Paul then said, "On the subject of the AA we thought we would probably be calling on their services this week at some point but it's turned out to be earlier than we anticipated… we haven't even had a can of lager yet."

Steve dropped us near the city centre and thanked us wholeheartedly for bailing him out. Maybe if you believe in fate you would say his good deed of picking us up was meant to be; allowing us to help him and prevent a mightily expensive and stressful episode for him breaking down alone without cover. It was a great feeling to know his generosity had allowed us to repay him. It was also a comedic start to the adventure.

Cardiff, Wales

Cardiff is a port city in South Wales at the junction of the River Taff and the Severn Estuary. It was declared the capital of Wales in 1955. Unbelievably, Wales did not have an official capital before this date, at least not in the eyes of the ruling government of the United Kingdom and elsewhere. Welsh history however, dates back much further than England's and the United Kingdom's, as does its difficult and distinctive language. Many people I meet on my world travels, on learning a little about Wales from me, regularly tend to ask, "So are the languages *(Welsh and English)* similar… like Spanish and Portuguese or the Scandinavian tongues?" The answer is that they couldn't be more different. They are both Indo-European but that's where the similarities end. English is a modern form of a Germanic language imported by the Anglo-Saxons post Roman rule from 500AD. Welsh is a modern form of an ancient Celtic language used by the original Britons of past millennia. They evolved on totally different trajectories. The letters K, Q, V, X and Z are not included in the Welsh alphabet but are sometimes found in borrowed words. Here are some examples of how different the languages are:

Gwdihw – Owl
Smwddio – Ironing (Clothes)

Chwyrligwgan – Merry-go-round
Clatsio – Fighting
Sglodion – Chips
Swmpus – Awesome
Clecs – Telling tales

Cardiff grew from a small town into a major industrial port city with the explosion of coal mining in the Welsh Valleys. A burial chamber shows that humans were inhabiting the wider area by at least 6000 BC, predating Stonehenge and the Great Pyramid of Giza by around 1,500 years. Cardiff Castle was built in 1081 and the original Roman fort is still visible in parts of the outer wall. In 1404 Owain Glyndwr, the Rebel Prince of Wales, burnt the town to the ground and claimed the castle for his crown. Ironically the capital now has a statue of Glyndwr in the town hall. The price of British coal was once determined in the market of Cardiff and the first ever million-pound deal was struck there in 1907.

Notable people to hail from Cardiff include: Author **Roald Dahl**, Actor **Ioan Gruffudd** (*Fantastic 4, King Arthur, Titanic, Hornblower*), Famous Sportsmen – **Ryan Giggs**, **Colin Jackson**, **Gareth Bale**. Musicians include: **Ivor Novello** (yes from the prize), **Shirley Bassey**, **Charlotte Church** and of course the legendary **Shakin' Stevens**.

It was already mid-afternoon and wanting to make up for our delay, we headed straight for a lane near the busy city train station. It was Friday night and some of the rugby crowd would be arriving for the night ready for an early start the next day; prime begging environment. We found a wall to slump against and I set to the task of making a begging sign from some local cardboard. Within minutes we were approached by an adversary. An extremely gaunt, pale and weathered looking man, carrying a can of potent lager, approached us with an irate look on his face and challenged us, "Ow, what are ew doing… are you *begging* here?" he rasped. The way he said 'begging' was in a surprised manner, as though we wouldn't dare have the cheek to be doing it here. Tramp 2 looked up at him and in a sarcastic manner said, "No mate, just waiting for a train." The lad muttered something to himself and was extremely disgruntled as he scorned at us, "You're on my patch, you better leave or there'll be trouble."

'Angry Boy' must've ran off to tell tales to his master because a minute later we were approached by another likely looking character, 'Tracksuit Tom the Tooth'. He paced towards us menacingly and was also carrying a can of booze. Tom was a little bigger than the first lad and appeared a lot more aggressive and assertive. He had a similar taste in super strength lager as 'Angry Boy' and no doubt super strength drugs too. Whilst introducing himself we noticed he only had one tooth left in his mouth. Tom was intent on a deeper chat than our first challenger.

"This is our patch lads, we have a system and an agreement between all the others. I don't recognise ew so can see you have made a mistake and not in the know."

We enquired about his system and he had no qualms about launching into an explanation about it. "Him over there (Angry Boy) sits there head bowed and feeling sorry for himself whilst begging. We make him look run down and scruffy with a blanket to get extra sympathy and then I'm the smart one 'coz I've got the tracksuit see (he started showing off his navy blue matching Adidas tracksuit). He sits there and makes em feel sad and then I approach them and catch them off guard by asking them outright for money. Most people get flustered with me in their face and just give me some money. I'm the smart one see, coz I got the tracksuit see (again pointing at it like it wasn't obvious)."

Tom conducted a now familiar routine we'd come to expect from fellow beggars and started interrogating us about who we were, what our story was and where we were from. We told him we were from Carmarthen due to the fierce rivalry between Swansea and

Cardiff which runs deeper than sporting differences. We felt there was no need to aggravate our position further whilst on the streets here. I felt that the level of aggression and threat we were already experiencing in Cardiff was a considerable amount more fierce than anything we encountered during our week in Swansea; definitely more cut throat. With this in mind and not really fancying starting the week with a fight we packed up to shuffle on.

Walking away Paul giggled and said, “That Trackie Tom the Tooth implied that they were like some kind of highly trained, military begging team.”
I agreed and said, “I don’t know how much he knows about Special Ops my boy, but he clearly knows a lot about Special Brew.”

Cardiff has a well renowned area of town in the heart of the nightlife called ‘Chippy Alley’. It is a lane approximately 100 metres long containing kebab shops, burger joints and general late night drunk food outlets. The uneven floor is covered in urine, vomit, blood and the heart-breaking evidence of a drunken reveller spilling a full tray of greasy food. It is frequently the scene of fights, arrests, copulation and people acting like dickheads. Inhibitions and rational thinking are abandoned at the entrance, so making it the perfect place to relieve people of their change.

I hadn’t spent much time there myself over the years so when we sat down halfway along it, I was surprised to see a Five Guys burger bar and a seedy adult shop placed metres from each other. It was amusing to watch the burger snobs look down on us as we transferred their looks of judgement onto the shifty blokes ghosting into the sex shop. Our spot was at a T-junction halfway along the lane that jutted into a modern bar quarter. It was a great spot to be visible to pedestrians from all three angles. Whilst sat begging, the following interactions occurred:
- We received a £10 note from a well-dressed ‘spray tan man’ and 6p from a lad in skinny jeans.

- Our military profile had attracted the attention of a young, serving Royal Marine who challenged our credentials and appeared dubious about them. He grilled me about my service and I eventually explained that I was a serving Sergeant and gave him the Trampface spiel. He became a little more reserved on hearing this information and moved on. (A few years later I had this same lad on a course that I was Chief Instructor for. It was to train and prepare Marines for promotion and he approached me at the start of the week and said "Colours, I think we've met before…").

- A drive by from a police patrol car resulting in the passenger PC leaning out the window and saying, "Please don't tell me you're Paras lads?" We confirmed that we weren't, and he said, "Have a nice day," and drove off.

- A lad called Martin who seemed to have ants in his pants stopped to chat and told us he is also homeless. He then offered us his library card so we could have a place of refuge. We declined his offer citing that we couldn't deprive him of his membership and he replied, "Don't worry lads, I've got six of them."

- A chat and hugs from some girls from Peru.

- A girl who had clearly had a bad run in with pigeons previously in life as she was sprinting around in an animated fashion trying to boot them; all the time shouting, "Move or I'll kick ew bleeding head off."

- Our first guilt-ridden encounter approached in the form of a girl called Leanne. She had a look of sorrow on her face and was on the phone to a chap called Ian who helps homeless people from a military background. She skipped between talking to him and passing the phone to us and after a while we couldn't keep up the pretence anymore. Our guilt got the better of us and the questions were getting too serious. We had no wish to waste these people's time so we quietly explained the Trampface mission to them.

- 2 x cigarettes were offered to us which we declined… Calais 'Bum a Fag Man' would be turning in his grave.

We were surprised that we were the only beggars on this patch considering its high footfall and loose attitude of the frequenters. I also thought that the passing police patrols may be less friendly to well-known beggars/troublemakers than they were. Our coffers, aka upturned desert hat, were filling up nicely thanks to the tipsy Friday afternoon revellers but we decided to change tact. Begging was nothing new to us, we desired to try something different. A few of the other beggars and passers-by had alerted us to the existence of a drop-in centre in town; its purpose was to support the homeless and desperate, a category which we fitted perfectly into.

The Huggard Centre was a short walk from Chippy Alley and looked to be a fairly spacious building. We entered a courtyard through some large and imposing steel gates and immediately became flanked on both sides by some intimidating looking addicts. There was no doubt the centre would house a regular crowd of cliques and known faces and we stuck out instantly. One girl said, "Hello lads," in an upbeat manner and this brought instant attention and looks of dislike towards us from her collection of male admirers. Undeterred, we pushed through the courtyard to the building entrance and edged through a more tightly packed group of men; all eyeballing us.

In the reception area we were greeted by a scene from a hybrid of *The Hangover* and *Dawn of the Dead.* A hollow square of chairs presented a collection of bodies slumped with beer cans all around them. It was unusual to see drinking being allowed in a drop-in centre; maybe it *wasn't* allowed but just too difficult to prevent. We waited awkwardly for our turn to chat with the staff whilst shouting, arguing and pushing erupted around us. A calm looking man in his thirties started a conversation with us and remarked on Tramp 2's desert combat trousers. He told us that his grandfather was in the British Army during 'the war' and the lad had great respect for the Forces. "Oh yea, is he still serving?" Paul joked and the lad replied, "Umm no, I don't think so," in a serious manner. I had to contain my snigger and embarrassment at him not realising the joke.

We checked in with the friendly and helpful staff and they took our details. Our cover story was deployed about being evicted in

Swansea and now tramping towards London for work. We gave our real names but provided no address of course. The staff told us to take a seat and mingle if we wished and we were given positive news that we had been placed on a waiting list for a floor space that night. It wouldn't be so positive for them when they heard us talking shit and laughing all night followed by Tramp 2's snoring. We were informed that every day around this time the centre conducts a clean-up and all occupants are encouraged to help; if they do so then they are rewarded with free meal vouchers. We lost the race to the cleaning cupboard by a mile to the now re-energised, booze fuelled residents. I whispered to Paul, "I bet they haven't moved that fast since Special Brew was on sale."

The place was clearing out for a few hours and the residents started to unplug their phones from the wall chargers and prepare to reluctantly leave. We were told by the staff to report back at 8:30pm, at which point we would be told if we had been allocated a space for the night. It was an exciting prospect, thinking about a new experience and witnessing what happens at night in a homeless hostel/shelter and we bounded off in high spirits to fill the time with some more begging.

Later on, we mustered back outside the high metal gates of the Huggard Centre and awaited news. There was a large gaggle of addicts outside and other healthier looking rough sleepers. The system would entail a staff member coming out and reading names of people that had been accepted. It wasn't done in one fell swoop, but more trickle fed every 10-20 minutes or so. Dribs and drabs of the chosen ones would be called and gradually the group outside got smaller. But the smaller it got the more agitated the outcasts became when it looked increasingly like they weren't getting in. A lot of them appeared to be in a real sorry state and I wondered how they would cope with being left out on the streets alone, especially with the morale blow of missing out on shelter. Some probably allowed themselves to get in such a state in the belief they would be secure for the night.

I had absolutely no faith that we would get called. If these seasoned visitors were getting snubbed, there's no way two new arrivals from out of town were getting in. Plus, I'm sure the staff realised we were a lot more capable of a night in the elements than the others. One guy had been spark out on the floor for the whole time we'd been there, not moved once… even when his friends had tried to rouse him. He was in a sorry state and I worried if he was going to make it through the night. One older guy with a Gandalf beard was walking around in circles, looking at the floor and talking to himself, just like the great wizard himself deliberating over something. However, if you caught his eye, when he looked up occasionally he would launch into an unwarranted torrent of abuse at you. I got caught a couple of times, I just couldn't help but peek at him the crazy old fool.

Despite the growing tension we struck up a conversation with a lad of Mongolian descent who had gravitated towards us. Julian was friendly, mild mannered and in his mid-twenties. He had the smooth skin of a baby face, black hair and was smartly dressed in a set of clean trousers and jacket. Julian appeared intelligent, aware and not under the influence of anything so I wondered why he was there. He was happy to open up and told us that he currently had a job but had relapsed into his crippling gambling addiction and was now homeless as a result. On payday for the last couple of months he had withdrawn the majority of his money and gambled it away, leaving him with rent arrears and finally eviction. We chatted easily and we found ourselves laughing when he started proudly showing us videos of his hero Genghis Khan on his smartphone, via YouTube. He was very proud of his Mongolian heritage but his accent was more 'Made in Essex' than East Asia.

The final call for places came and we were disappointed that our earlier charm offensive on the staff hadn't worked, even though it was predicted we wouldn't get in. Mongolian Julian hadn't made the cut either and we trudged off together in the drizzling rain towards town. Julian seemed more prepared than the others and admitted he didn't expect to get a spot. He proudly showed us his four-season sleeping bag and sports holdall full of kit to sustain him. I was glad he was in a good position to take care of himself and hoped we'd see him again as we wished him well.

Before we had moved off from the centre, a member of staff had shouted, "Don't go too far, we may get an opening." Even though it seemed there was a chance of a place at the Huggard, we had decided to let it go for the night and just crack on ourselves. It had been worth a shot and the experience was good anyway… who knows, maybe we would get lucky another night! Our sights were set once again on Chippy Alley. The drinkers would be out in force now and we hoped they would take pity on our sorry little faces. Our bellies were rumbling; despite collecting some decent begging money, we had decided to hold out through a little hardship and see if we could get fed from a direct source.

We resumed our position near the adult shop and over the following two hours we sat getting gradually colder as we felt a rapid drop in the temperature. We did start to become humbled by people's (drunken) generosity and received the following engagements:

- Several other homeless people approached us and each had an equally elaborate and sympathy inducing story about being on the streets. At times some of them seemed as well rehearsed as a Broadway thespian.
- Before the cash started flowing, a flower seller lady, the type that pesters any man walking with a female to buy a rose, walked past and looked into our empty hat. She then shrieked through laughter, "Haha you've got no money."
- A young blonde girl and her mother approached peacefully and her mother ushered her forward with encouragement to give us a bag of chips and a can of Pepsi.
- A Portuguese girl gave us a hug.
- A tall lad from the Dutch Army gave us £10.

- An ex Sgt Major gave us £5.
- 4 x Cherry Bakewells from an open box were gifted to us.
- We gleefully accepted 1 x tray of curry and chips to share.

Chippy Alley had come up trumps and we packed up to move off and find somewhere to sleep. Before finding anywhere suitable we spotted a busy Burger King and took the opportunity for some snap begging. We hastily plonked ourselves against the glass window next to the entrance and quickly found we had unwanted company. A skinny girl with a haggard face and no teeth was tearing towards us in a state of absolute delirium. She lurched over the top of us and started aggressively berating us. "You fuckers are not from Cardiff, ew are weekend beggars from out of town. I can't get any money because of fuckers like you *and* you've got a sign… a fucking sign! Who do ew think ew are with ew sign. Ew can just fuck off, ew and ew sign, go on."

For some reason she had a right beef with the sign, she wouldn't shut up about it and was mocking us for having one, like we were some kind of pathetic losers. We were mostly just taking it and smiling at another story for the blog but then she really got to me. She kept on and on and wouldn't go away and I was getting a bit fed up when she then grabbed our sign and ripped it in half. I don't know why, but it infuriated me and I almost lost my temper right there, she had no right to grab our stuff like that. The stupid git then ran over to a couple of police officers to grass us up for begging, even showed them our sign. Tramp 2 looked at me and said, "Jesus, she hates signs more than pigeon girl hates birds." I had had enough and ran over to salvage our sign, it was the principle of it and I ripped it out of her hands and told her to "Fuck off".

She kept on taunting us from a distance and was laughing and mocking us, including proclaiming to passers-by, "Look at them losers with a sign." The police did nothing and the manager from Burger King came out and apologised to us for the trouble, "She's a nightmare lads, sorry about that. I've got no problem with you begging here and I'll grab you some more cardboard." We received 2 x burger meals from a reveller before the manager re-emerged with some boxes and 2 x XL bacon double cheeseburgers for our inconvenience. Unbelievable! "Legend," Tramp 2 said.

Our options for a place to sleep were pretty poor. Although there was a large park near the castle it had far too many open areas and any sheltered ones were in close proximity to a path. We did an uneasy loop and as we had so often found on our missions, that first night we found ourselves plagued with doubt and paranoia of being watched. It usually took a couple of days of tiredness and familiarity to settle into sleeping anywhere but we wouldn't be afforded the latter as our plan was to move to a new town each day. Eventually we crawled halfway under a sparse bush near a cottage and the old castle's boundary wall. It was quiet now but come the morning the road the other side of it would be hectic and our position open to any onlooker.

It was 3am so we would only have a few hours of darkness to rest but I doubted we would get much. We settled down and agreed it was a cracking first day. From breaking down with Steve to meeting Mongolian Julian and £76.43 in begging cash. Our encounter with 'Tracksuit Tom the Tooth' had left a bitter taste in my mouth. Those guys were clearly professional beggars with no desire to get off the streets when they can con people out of money for their fix. A lot of people put all homeless people in the same bracket but those idiots give a bad name to those who are desperate to get back into society. They also suck up the support and benefits that should be directed to people wishing to get off the streets. No doubt they have mental health issues but at what point do we just allow them to do what they want and take from others but not give back. We had definitely seen a more cut throat and sinister side to life on the streets than witnessed in Swansea. Maybe that's the only way to survive in a big city with more ruthless competition.

We had absolutely no idea what tomorrow held apart from chancing some begging in the surreal crowd of a couple of hundred thousand people out drinking for the rugby. We did however, know what we were having for breakfast… 2 cold XL bacon double cheeseburgers. We hoped Steve had made it home without further incident and prayed Mongolian Julian had found a safe spot to rest. With excited thoughts about where the next day may take us we signed off with our first nightly ritual of this year's adventure.

"Night night Hiker 1."
"Night, night Hiker 2."

HITCHHIKE DAY 2

"A Free Game, Train and Shelter from the Rain"

First light brought noise and the close proximity of inconsiderate morning commuters to our position. The wall we were laying in the lee of was high and unscalable from our position on the grass. However, the opposite side had a pavement and busy road running parallel which allowed anyone to peer over. Our corner position now looked across the wide-open park and we would be easily visible to anyone walking through it. It was early, but we were awake and would gain no benefit from hanging around. A quick scan of our position in the daylight highlighted that Steve's speedometer needle wasn't the only one that had dropped yesterday… we were surrounded by silver cooking up trays and hypodermic needles used for the injection of heroin. The thought of being jabbed by one whilst on the floor, was almost as alarming as the thought of the users returning to the position whilst we were occupying it asleep.

Our stashed burgers from the night before were dispatched for breakfast as we walked towards the central library to type out our daily update. In Swansea we had registered at the library in order to take advantage of the free Internet terminals during the seven days. For this current mission it would be time-consuming and a waste of effort doing this in each town so we had brought a mini laptop that we could use in any free WiFi spot. However, today we could lord it in front of a full-size PC in the comfortable surrounds of Cardiff Library, for we had been given one of Martin's six library membership cards the day before. This also allowed us to charge our phones.

I sat at the terminal and typed in the membership number along with the password that Martin had taped to the back of the card. "Incorrect password" flashed back at me, so I tried it a couple more times but to no avail. We sighed at this delay to our routine and concluded that one of us would have to approach the desk. "Go on mush, you are better at talking people round than I am," I said persuasively. Tramp 2 rolled his eyes, snatched the card from me and approached the desk. He explained that he had forgotten his password and enquired about the best way to help with his predicament; he got in return a very undesirable answer from the attendant, "It's your date of birth in six digit format." Paul, thinking on his feet said, "What happens if I've tried that but it didn't work, can you just reset it to a new one?" The lady frowned at him and took the card from him, she then said, "Look, I'll try it for you. What's your date of birth Mr Lewis?"

I couldn't help but sit there and laugh at Tramp 2 squirming at being caught out and I could sense him cursing me. The lady at the desk looked up at him after receiving no answer and said, "Mr Lewis, date of birth?" Paul couldn't keep it up anymore and had no other option but to admit to her that it wasn't his card and that he had been given it by another homeless man. The lady gave him a playful look of scorn and said sympathetically, "OK, well I'll log you guys in for today but you will have to apply if you want to come back again." Tramp 2 returned and gave me a pained look, I said, "See mush, that's why I suggested you should go."

We smashed out our first update in good time whilst laughing and thinking back to Tom the Tooth and Mongolian Julian. The nice lady at the library was going to be pestered one last time by us before we left. It was my turn so I approached her and said, "Could we borrow some Sellotape please? Our begging sign got ripped up by an angry girl last night and although we have some more cardboard we are quite fond of this sign and would like to salvage it. Waste not want not as we Swansea tramps say." She obliged, with a friendly shake of her head, and we spent a couple of minutes knelt on the floor making essential repairs to our sign. Surely an unusual sight for the Saturday morning library visitors.

Our plan for the day was clear, take full advantage of the boozed-up rugby crowd who would be plentiful in numbers and out drinking heavily far earlier than normal. Although this *was* Wales, so probably not that surprisingly early! Even though this plan would tie us down in Cardiff longer than we'd have liked, it was a trade-off for the chance to experience begging in the midst of a huge influx of people. Hitching would then be attempted once the game had kicked off and the crowds were otherwise occupied. Wales were playing Italy in the final match of the Six Nations championship at the Millennium Stadium, which was a mere couple of hundred metres away from our spot in Chippy Alley.

The lane was full of rugby fans and the coast seemed to be clear of police and other beggars, which really surprised us. Our familiar spot around halfway down opposite the T junction was initially hindered ~~in its suitability~~. This was due to groups of people stood munching chips right in front of us and blocking us from the sight of the wandering crowds. Once one small group had done it, it seemed to become the official gathering place and pockets of others followed. Tramp 2 soon came up with a plan to solve our dilemma. "I noticed this morning whilst packing up that I'd knelt in some shit last night my boy, I can smell it on me. I'm going to use that and old Tom the Tracksuit Tooth's fool proof plan to sort this out." He then proceeded to stand right next to all the chip eaters in turn and ask them if he could "pinch a chip" or if they could "spare some change". Within no time at all they had all dispersed with looks of disgust on their faces at the intrusion. Tramp 2 returned to me and with a beaming smile and said, "Tom the Tooth may have the tracksuit my boy, but I've got the dogshit. Well, I hope it was dogshit… not smackhead shit."

The cash flow was surprising slow initially and we begrudged the fact that we had been passed by an overwhelmingly large amount of people and received not a penny. The ratio of cash to footfall compared to the night before was at extreme odds. We consoled ourselves with the fact that sometimes that's just the way it goes and it would soon pick up. We hoped so, as we had taken a risk on hanging around for the rugby instead of hitching straight on. Then something amazing happened…

A man in his forties walked past with his son, who was in his early teens, and was looking inquisitively at us whilst also slowing his pace. He was dressed smartly but comfortably, kind of like an off-duty businessman, if you know what I mean? I could see the cogs turning in his head and the moment that he reached a decision point, influencing him to turn around after ten metres or so. He approached us purposely and his son had the expression, "What are you doing Dad?" etched on his face. He paused in front of us as we looked up at him and he said, "I'm guessing you are ex-forces lads, I am also so can always spot a fellow squaddie." His next action stunned us, he crouched down, placed two shiny tickets into our begging hat and said, "Here you go lads, enjoy the match."

He had given us two tickets for the international rugby match that afternoon… gold dust basically. It was a sell-out and the final game of the tournament, there would be little chance of getting a ticket if you had tried. We were stunned for a moment at this act of kindness and looked at each other in amazement. I came to my senses and joined Tramp 2 in saying thanks but that we couldn't possibly take someone's tickets from them. The gentleman assured us that it was fine, "They were initially for the wife and my youngest son, but they have decided to go to the cinema instead. So, they are all yours lads, don't worry." He offered a further gesture which showed that he really did just want to help us, "Feel free to sell them if you want lads, probably get a good price for them now. Use the cash to sort yourselves out for the night, no worries lads, honestly." It was very humbling to hear him say that and I replied that we would be delighted to go to the match and enquired whether we would be sat next to him. He replied that we wouldn't, we would be next to some of his other friends and Paul gave him some stick, "Oh yea, embarrassed to sit next to a couple of stinking tramps is it?" He was flustered for a moment before noticing us both smiling back at him.

We were both revelling at this astonishing incident when we had a moment of anxiousness at the sight of the man running back towards us with a look of regret on his face. "Shit, he wants the tickets back my boy," Paul said. The gentleman approached and composed himself, he then said, "I'm really sorry lads," which made my heart flutter before he continued, "I've given you the wrong tickets, they are for the seats I planned to sit in." We put our most serious faces on and replied bluntly, "What tickets mate?" He paused for a moment, scrutinising our faces for a reaction but was met with two straight faced and unflinching tramps. We then laughed in unison and said, "Sorry Sir, these tickets are actually non-refundable or transferrable ones. We will require a £5 handling fee in order to process the transaction. All transactions are final and we only accept cash."

We all laughed again and Paul gave him some more stick about giving us the cheap seats and panicking once he realised he'd given us his premium ones. We swapped tickets, he shook our hands once more and we wished him well.

Shocked but delighted is how I would describe our mood at the feel of two pristine match tickets in our possession. We discussed how unexpected the whole thing was but in reality, it was exactly the type of thing Trampface had come to experience. We were regretful that we hadn't even caught the man's name but were comforted that we could torture his friends for two hours at the rugby and find out! It was a fantastic gesture and heart-warming to be on the receiving end of it. Funny how such an interaction can make you feel elated and carefree whilst sitting in the cold, on a urine stained floor whilst attracting dirty looks. Our joyous mood was soon about to go up a notch…

"Here you go lads, a few quid to get some scran later. I was a Navy man myself and you boys have served I take it?" We confirmed that we had and asked the Matelot if he was going to the game with his son who he had in tow. He sighed and replied in a downbeat manner, "Yes lads, I've just paid well over the odds for a couple of tickets from the street touts. Oh well." Paul couldn't resist and piped up straight away, "Nightmare mush, you should've tried a spot of begging. Ten minutes ago our afternoon consisted of getting a few coins in return for drunken abuse but now we are heading to the game. We'll see you in there… where are ew sitting?"

The bloke laughed at us in a mocking fashion, clearly believing there was no way we could've acquired a couple of tickets from begging. Paul assured him that we weren't joking and brandished our tickets for him to inspect. The guy was flabbergasted and had a look of spite on his face, not helped by Tramp 2 laughing and after finding out where the guy was sitting saying, "We've got better seats than you too mush. At least you know better for next time." It was safe to say the man was not impressed and almost certainly now regretted giving us some money.

We'd made the decision to put in another hour or so of begging, the tickets for the match were free but the food and beer wouldn't be! Our original plan was to start hitching once the crowd dispersed and the match kicked off. However, our plans had now changed meaning a hefty delay and darkness, but we felt it was worthwhile to go with the flow. Our spot was opposite a Five Guys burger joint and we were giggling at the dirty looks we were getting from the run-of-the-mill security guard acting the tough guy in front of all the tipsy girls. Tramp 2 leaned over and joked, "I wonder if it's called Five Guys in honour of him, he's got enough chins for five Italian opera singers." I giggled and replied, "Yea, maybe we should ask him to donate us a 'tenor'?" We both shook our heads at the poor standard of the pun but were still left laughing uncontrollably nonetheless.

Kick-off was 2:30pm and over the next hour we received a heavy influx of loose change, banter, food and drunken hugs. The crowd was in a party mood and didn't fail to entertain us. A couple of hard looking, shaved headed men approached us menacingly and asked if we were ex-forces. After we had confirmed that we were they asked what unit I was in (having noticed my Royal Marines badge sewn on my jumper). I gave some vague answers in order to string them along out of interest and one of them lost his temper and snapped at me, "I asked you what Commando unit you were in, I'm sick of seeing fuckers like you exploiting people's love for veterans. You ever heard of stolen valour?" I scoffed back at his verbal attack and gave him my service number, units served in and my four operational tours of Iraq and Afghanistan. I then asked him what unit he had served in, to which he somewhat now sheepishly said, "29 Commando" This is an army unit who do a section of the Royal Marine Commando tests in order to validate them working with us. I then left him with a parting shot, "Some may call you a rubber dagger *(a slur in reference to them only doing 10 weeks commando training compared to 32)* but not me mate. Nice to meet you though, have a good day."

Happy with our haul and excited for the match we packed up and set off through the throng of supporters. The routine bag check at the gate turned out to be quite a spectacle when we arrived. Onlookers and guards alike were bewildered at the sight of two tramps unrolling their sleeping bags, toothbrush and spare pants! Safely inside we were directed towards our seats and identified some space behind the rear row to stash our bags. Security came rushing over and we were told in no uncertain terms to never leave our bags unattended due to security threats. After our ticking off I offered Tramp 2 a potential plan, "If we leave our bags unattended towards the end of the match we could head to the concourse and set up a begging station, complete with sign. Then we could take full advantage of the bottleneck of 72,000 people with heavy pockets."

Settled into our seats, we eagerly awaited finding out who the friends of our ticket benefactor were. An attractive lady to our left started chatting with us and we soon discovered that she, along with her husband and two daughters were them. Margaret said that she had briefly been told that she would be sitting next to a couple of homeless blokes but hadn't got the full story. Our kind ticket sponsor was a man named Arwyn Watkins, a Michelin Star chef from a town called Welshpool. He is the founder of an apprentice college for aspiring young Welsh chefs called Cambrian Training. We were now even more humbled by him and his actions. We joked with the family, "Arwyn came back to swap the tickets because he didn't want to sit with you guys but would rather lumber you with two stinking tramps for the duration of the match." At the time of writing this Arwyn had been awarded the honour of an OBE.

We decided to stick to the cover story with Margaret and retold it with vigour, once again emphasising that we were heading to London to find work. The game was brilliant, Wales crushed Italy and our new friends were great company. We posed for a couple of pics, of course, and hatched a new plan for getting out of town.

The game had seriously delayed our escape from the city to pastures new and we had to be honest with ourselves about our chances of hitching a lift. It was dark and most vehicles would be full of fans desperate to get clear of the city chaos as soon as possible. Our chances were probably as low as ever in scoring a ride. I had an idea.

The match day chaos could work to our favour in another way. There would be a mass exodus via the train station and my previous experience of this brought the knowledge that it was unlikely any ticket barriers would be enforced. There were several massive queues lined up in front of boards indicating a destination and once the train was ready the guards would open the gate and usher everyone straight through. The sheer volume of people made it undesirable to check tickets and cause delay and disruption. Maybe we could hitch a lift with a different kind of transport.

We joined the queue full of confidence about slipping through without payment. I started chatting with two elegant, elderly ladies from Bath and engaged in some playful two-way flirting whilst also rolling out the cover story. The queue became quite rowdy with pushing and shoving so we explained to the ladies that we would protect them and we did indeed shield them from several violent surges. Once we had guided them safely to the platform, we said goodbye and one of the ladies had tears in her eyes as she hugged me and presented me with a £20 note. She was clearly upset and wished us well with trying to get to London. We walked away and the guilt hit me like a brick. I consoled myself by reasoning that it showed the good in people and allowed this nice lady to ponder on a real issue faced in society.

Behind us in the queue was a well-built man who had joined in our conversation in a friendly and happy manner. Martin was a heavily set ex-professional rugby player who went on to tell us tales about playing with some of the rugby greats including Adrian Hadley, Mark Ring and Glen Webbe. Martin was in his fifties and of African origin. He told us that he had been adopted when six months old from Ghana, along with his sister, by a white couple from South Wales. It was amazing to sit and be on the receiving end of someone else's tales for once but Martin's tales also had an element of sadness. Through tears, he told us that he considered himself very lucky to have been adopted by two very kind and special people and that he had grown up with his fellow adopted siblings which included a boy from India and a girl whose full origins were unknown. It was truly humbling and amazing to hear Martin's story and we traded humorous stories as well as the heartfelt ones.

I was disappointed to leave Martin and had very much enjoyed meeting him. We took his phone number and wished him all the best in life. Not wanting to push our luck from the free train ride we decided to hop off at Bristol before the train became quieter which would draw our fraudulent selves into the spotlight. Our destination was Bristol Temple Meads and our luck was definitely about to be tested.

Bristol, England

Bristol is a city and county in South West England. It sits in a pivotal position, with London to the east, Wales to the west and England's second city of Birmingham to the north. It has a population of over 450,000 people and a famous zoo! Its Old English name translates to 'Place at the bridge' and it has heavy evidence of Iron Age hill forts and Roman villas in the surrounding areas. Bristol fell behind in the race for dominance due to the rapid rise of the industrial revolution in several key cities in the north.

The city enjoys a rich maritime history as the starting place for early voyages of exploration to the New World. In 1497, John Cabot became the first European, since the Vikings, to land on mainland North America (although there are Welsh claims to earlier landings). In 1499, William Weston became the first Englishman to lead an exploration to North America. A regrettable fact for Bristol is that during the height of the slave trade more than 2,000 ships passed through, carrying an estimated 500,000 people from Africa into slavery in the Americas.

Bristol has the largest circulating community currency in the UK, the Bristol pound, which is one for one with Sterling. Between one third and a half of the population died from the spread of Black Death in 1348. The famous Victorian engineer, Brunel, is associated with the city and he pioneered the Great Western Railway between Bristol and London. Bristol was heavily bombed by the Lufftwaffe during World War II with nearly 100,000 buildings damaged. It was also bombed by the IRA in 1974 and 1978.

Apart from the people mentioned earlier, famous Bristolians include: **Sir Humphrey Davy** (inventor of laughing gas and the miners' safety lamp). **Princess Caraboo** (the fraudulent foreign princess who appeared out of the blue talking a strange language. She was actually a cobbler's daughter from Devon). **Billy Butlin** (founder of the infamous holiday camps). **Cary Grant** (world famous actor). **JK Rowling** (Harry Potter author). **Banksy** (controversial and anonymous graffiti artist with sales in the millions). **David Prowse** (Darth Vader). **Stephen Merchant** (Office, Extras). **Keith Floyd**, the legendary TV chef whose notorious drinking habits have inspired many a Trampface night out!

Our excitement from the match had caused us to overlook one important detail, not all stations would be in the same disarray as Cardiff and have their barriers dropped. The exit at Bristol was blocked by a line of intimidating and disheartening ticket barriers sporting big red crosses. Paul met my look of frustration and said, "Looks like this isn't going to be easy my boy."

Tramp 2 didn't hesitate in trying to resolve the situation by walking up to the lady steward stood near the barriers and saying, "Ow, how do I get out of here?"
Steward Lady, "Put your ticket in the barrier."
Tramp 2, "Ohh I left it on the train."
Steward Lady, "OK, where have you come from?"
Tramp 2, assessing that the closer the station the less the fee if we were rumbled, blurted out, "Bristol Parkway."
Steward Lady, "How much did it cost?"
Tramp 2, being speculative, "A fiver."
Steward Lady, "No it didn't as it is our pound saver stop and only £1."
We were completely busted and at a loss for a way out. The lady could clearly smell blood and laid out our limited options, "It's an £80 fine or I call the police."
Tramp 2, "Typical gormless jobsworth, we are homeless, have a bit of compassion."
Steward Lady. "Pay up or it's the police."

Tramp 2 displayed his bacon allergy and vaulted the barrier before calmly walking away. The gormless wonder then hit the red button which produced 4 x British Transport Police bursting out of their office. She was screaming out instructions making out that the great train robbery had been reincarnated. Two officers chased Tramp 2 and seemed to be surprised that he wasn't running away; he turned around calmly and spoke to them. The other two came towards me and adopted a cautious demeanour when nearing my position. The officers started grilling me and I could see, by peering over their shoulder, that Tramp 2 was receiving the same treatment. A knowing smile from him confirmed to me that he was being awkward and sticking to the story about leaving our tickets on the train, just like I was.

The lady jobsworth kept on butting in which appeared to be exasperating the officers. She then angered me by saying that I'd tried to jump the barrier. I calmly explained to the officers that if I had attempted to jump the barrier then I wouldn't still be stood on the platform as it was hardly a super human feat to achieve. I gave the lady an unimpressed look and shook my head. The officers seemed to be getting irritated by her also and she resorted to threats saying she would check the CCTV at the other station but we both stood our ground and stuck to our story. She realised we weren't budging and made the mistake of trying to barter with us. Suddenly the £80 fine had been reduced to £3… if we gave our names and addresses. Paul replied, "Do you think we are stupid? Hand over our details so you can send us the original £80 fine? Good luck if we did, we are homeless as we have already explained."

The lady had had enough of the two stubborn tramps in front of her and acted like a spoilt teenager when she admitted defeat and said, "Officers, can you take them away and deal with it?" I had sensed a change in attitude once we had told the officers that we were homeless but they still reunited us on the platform side of the barriers and forcefully marched us away. We now feared the worst of course and expected to see the inside of a holding cell pretty soon. Our escorts led us into an official office and I crouched to sit down, ready for the impending processing to come. As my backside touched the chair the Sergeant in charge said, "Whoa lads, don't sit down you aren't staying?" We looked at each other in shock and then looked at the officer for clarity. He continued with, "We are taking you to the VIP entrance," and opened the rear door into the public car park. He then said, "That woman is an absolute nightmare, have a good night boys."

Free from our shackles, we laughed and gave ourselves an inflated compliment about the Trampface charm once again paying off. It was around 8pm so we didn't have a great deal of time to explore the bouncing homeless scene of Bristol. The corner of a building in the busy nightlife area was chosen to deploy our trusty cardboard cash cow. Within a few minutes our quiet spot had been transformed into a hive of activity and we were surrounded by a large group of enthusiastic mobile soup kitchen volunteers. Their presence was soon followed up with free loving hugs, soup and ham rolls. The cheerful volunteers then moved along and were replaced by a friendly young lady who offered us two cream turnovers. Next up, we were to be humbled by an attractive student girl who stopped and looked at us with compassion whilst putting her hand on her heart. She showed interest in our plight and said that she only had 70p on her but we were welcome to it and she was sorry she couldn't give us more. She was extremely downbeat and full of sorrow and gave us a warm embrace before parting with the words, "I really hope things turn out well for you lads."

After the young lady had left we had a moment of reflection about her compassion and emotions. Tramp 2 then said, "I think that kebab stand opposite has been cutting some strong onions my boy." I agreed, silently.

Our earlier decision to have a couple of beers at the rugby was due to our successful begging sessions. From a mere few hours begging over two days we were now in receipt of over £200 in cash. We would reimburse anything we spent to the charity as always but were also free to use it like a homeless person would. After all, the rugby tickets and cash we had earned were from people believing that we were legitimate tramps. These two tramps like beer but at this point we were knackered from little sleep and a busy day, so we decided to treat ourselves to a couple of bottles of water before trying to find somewhere to bed down.

Our energy levels weren't going to sustain a detailed scope of the area so we started scanning left, right, up, down and anywhere for somewhere to crash. It's a strange feeling not knowing if you are going to find a suitable place to sleep for the night. It's also not a very comforting thought that your idea of 'suitable' falls far short of most other people's perception. Our 'suitable' right there and then was a corner bank-like building, under renovation with scaffolding and a perimeter steel fence. Drops of rain were starting to fall and we assessed that the scaffolding would provide some protection from above, considering that we had not brought any overhead cover. "We'll be up and over that in a second my boy," was Paul's opinion on the building site's defences. I told him that in all honesty I was eyeing up crawling *under* the fence… "Ahh the difference between being 6"4 and 5"10."

We were stood in a trance, eyeing up our methods of entry, when we were approached by two ladies from North Devon who immediately asked, "Are you guys sleeping rough?"
I replied, "We are trying to, yes," and one then directly asked if it was for charity. I was a little bit perplexed by this and thought that she may have seen the Trampface page. We chatted briefly and she said that she just had a feeling from looking at us that we were doing it for charity, weird. They gave us £20 for the charity and moved off, allowing us to now jump the fence.

Once underneath the scaffolding we found a dusty doorway to park ourselves in but after an evaluation of the surface we realised the hard concrete floor would benefit from some padding. I was sure there would be some lying around in this busy city centre and volunteered to go in search. I rounded the corner of our building and realised that we didn't actually need to jump the fence after all, as there was a gap to slip through around the other side. I slipped out and went to track down some cardboard to enhance our squat for the night. Our position was mostly sheltered by the scaffolding above but due to its elevation, any gusting wind would cause the rain to drift underneath. However, the fence would easily shield us from prying eyes wandering around in the night.

We giggled whilst recapping the events of the day and jotted down the key points in my notepad, a now routine action for us so that we could refer to it when writing the update. We agreed that it had once again been a unique and entertaining day and wondered where our next destination would be. Our daily begging total amounted to £110.99 and two tickets worth £60 each face value. Jumping out from Steve's car in Cardiff had been a good call, but would our luck and judgement last the whole week? In our cold dark corner of a Bristol building site we attempted to drift off to sleep.

"Night night Hiker 1."
"Night night, Hiker 2."

HITCHHIKE DAY 3

"Goodnight Mr Birkin"

The temperature dropped rapidly throughout the night and prevented an easy transition into sleep. Each time we drifted off, we would awake shivering badly, our thin jungle sleeping bags offered little insulation. Several times we were found to be huddling together closely to radiate some warmth between us. The position was cordoned off from view but was not buffered from the noise of constant traffic and noisy weekend revellers. We drifted off to sleep before first light and were confident of not being directly disturbed; the position was chosen with the fact in mind that the next morning was a Sunday. This suggested that workers were unlikely to turn up at the site on the day of rest.

Our assessment was wrong. I was startled to realise from my cocooned position on the deck that dust was now raining down from the creaking scaffold boards above. It was 7am and a large truck had transported a lively scaffold gang to the site who were all now nosily working above us. I felt a little mischief at the realisation that they didn't know we were there but I knew we would have to move soon or get rumbled still in our sleeping bags. We rapidly got up and were resigned to the fact that we would need to expose ourselves to the workers in order to exit the site. I shuffled my meagre belongings together and curiously looked around to weigh up our best route. We strode boldly towards the exit around the corner and received looks of bewilderment from the workers above. They froze in confusion and gawped at us until eventually one of them said, "Who the fuck are you two?"

Tramp 2 provided them with a smart and prompt answer and said, "We are undercover health and safety executives, just checking the site for safety and compliance. All seems to be in order, good effort boys… crack on." The men were scratching their heads, a couple of them even laughing when I confused them even more by asking,

"Do you know where the nearest Wetherspoons pub is lads? We have to write up our report about your site and we are gagging for eggs benedict and a pint." One of them, without saying a word, pointed to a building 20 metres away. Winner.

Our unexpected early start meant that we would get a good head start on the hitchhiking. Bristol has a busy route out of it called the M32 and we thought that it would be wise to get close to it. Out of interest and adventure, we decided to chance our luck on a few spots throughout town which actually turned out to bear some valuable information. A couple approached us and informed us that they were seasoned hitchhikers, "Lads, try the Shell garage down the road. It never fails, we use it all the time and you'll get a lift no problem." The guy said, whilst pointing down in the direction of a road leading off from the roundabout.

We followed the local advice and after locating the garage near a busy arterial road, deployed our sign which now said, "North and/or East." The initial signs were not promising and I began to doubt the credibility of the advice we had been given. We were afforded a distraction when two scruffy characters approached us whilst staggering and shouting obscenities. The male of the pair smashed a bottle of cider in front of us for no reason other than to try and antagonise us and the girl, who had boot polish for eyebrows, then asked us for some change. It wasn't a tactic we approved of and I told her we were homeless and unable to give her anything.

A further 20 fruitless minutes passed accompanied by blank stares and I wondered if we'd been given bad intelligence on purpose. The road sure was busy and so was the garage, so maybe it was just a matter of sticking it out. We were stood around 10 metres in front of the entrance which would allow customers pulling in for fuel to see us and mull over picking us up. Out of the corner of my eye I could see a solitary, young lady approaching us. I fidgeted uncomfortably as I wasn't sure why she would be approaching us; it did not seem likely to me that she would be offering a lift. The young lady surprised me by saying, "Hi lads, saw your sign. I'm going to Worcester if that is any good?" We smiled and accepted her kind offer. I was shocked that a lone female would offer to pick up two scruffy, rough looking men and felt an immediate respect for Kate for doing so. Gender no doubt plays a role in what type of people participate in hitchhiking but this was more about stature. Kate was short and slender and did no doubt believe that she could trust the two men jumping into her vehicle who could easily overpower her.

Kate had a very laid-back vibe and was clearly a believer in humanity. We chatted, and she explained that she had been visiting friends in Bristol for a rare break from her three-year-old twins. She carried the tell-tale signs of being a busy mother; dark rings around her eyes. We told her about Trampface and she told us that she is a full-time mum allowing her partner to work a mixture of gardening and driving jobs. Their home is Birmingham but they desire to move to Devon one day and allow their children to grow up near the countryside and coast. She was preaching to the choir and we both celebrated our childhood and current location living near the beach and the hills.

Kate was quizzed about our potential to get an interesting homeless experience in Worcester and returned with the verdict that we would be better advised to go elsewhere. One Royal Marine survival principle is to seek local knowledge, this particular local was convincing in her recommendation. Therefore, we asked to be dropped at a motorway services in order to try and get a ride to somewhere with a little more action. The location was Strensham Services near the Midlands and as we jumped out of Kate's small van Paul became excited, "Look there's a Cymru Coach over there, must be from South Wales and northbound." He exclaimed. We approached the driver's window which sported the predictable, chubby, balding man with a scowl on his face. Our request about room for two charming hitchhikers was met with a flat refusal… made even more dejecting when he justified it with, "No chance, I got a bus full of cheerleaders boys." With a creepy wink to boot.

A new angle needed to be approached so we set up near the services entrance with both our begging sign and hitching one. Cheeky and a bit greedy but it would be an experiment and we had to get some action somehow. Sunday afternoon would be busy at the services with people commuting back to work from the weekend. Some may have hangovers and the desire to wallow in self-loathing alone, some may have a long trek and would welcome the company. It wasn't the biggest or busiest service station around but maybe that was a positive as people wouldn't feel so rushed and disgruntled pushing through crowds. A more relaxed stroll into the services may cultivate a liberal attitude towards acts of kindness.

It seemed it *had* created a positive environment and a mere five minutes later we received a toot from a couple of lads in a Ford Focus. It was the same type of car we had been picked up, and broken down, in on Day 1. Rich and Will were well-spoken army officers on their way back to camp from weekend leave; they offered to drop us in Derby. We put our bags on our laps and settled in for the journey. I noticed some curious looks reflected back towards us from the driver's mirror and could sense some probing was to come. After some small talk the lads naturally quizzed us about our military appearance and I could tell they were suspicious of our ex-forces story. After playing along to see their reaction we gave them the truth and they laughed, saying that they knew there was something more to our story.

We traded stories from our service with the lads and told them about our near miss with a coachload of cheerleaders. Rich and Will looked at each other with wide eyes and were a little taken aback by it. Will then said, "We saw that group inside, I guess the driver didn't tell you that they were about 12 years old, did he? Old creep." The lads advised us that we'd be better placed in Nottingham as opposed to Derby, "A bit more pleasant and definitely more going on to be honest." Nottingham it was.

Nottingham, English Midlands, Maid Marian Country

Nottingham is in the East Midlands of England, it is a small but very famous city, mostly because of its association with Robin Hood. It regularly grosses over £1.5 billion from tourism and its two universities house over 60,000 students in a general population of 330,000. In 2015 it was named 'Home of English Sport' and possesses the oldest professional football club in the world, Notts County. It's old age name in Brythonic (related to Welsh) was *Tigguo Cobauc (Place of Caves)* and in modern Welsh is known as Y Ty Ogofog. When it came under the rule of a Saxon Chieftain named Snot it became hilariously (to me anyway) known as 'Snotingham'... literally *the town of snot people*. The traffic light was first invented in Nottingham by a high school student named John Peake Knight in 1866. He wanted a solution to the amount of people being killed on the roads and created a system with a revolving gas-powered red and green lantern.

Nottingham has the world's smallest cinema which can seat only 21 guests. It has the loudest clock bell in the country which can be heard seven miles away and is called 'Little John'. The pharmacy chain 'Boots' was born here in 1849 where a young apprentice named (Dr) Stewart Adams performed random trials of pain killing chemical substances. His only successful attempt was later named 'ibuprofen' which he tested on himself for a hangover (thanks mate). Gotham, the village responsible for the inspiration for Batman's hangout, resides in Nottinghamshire and Wollaton Hall was used as Wayne Manor in the 2012 film. Nottingham is the location of the only branch of the famous American restaurant Hooters in England... more on that in a bit.

It was already dark when the lads dropped us near a bridge. We cracked on with some begging but were soon approached by a fellow Tramp. He greeted us calmly and explained that our profile may help us out in the Hooters restaurant just down the road, "It's military discount night lads so you may get some concession... and attention." Being actively frugal guys, we decided we should go and try out this friendly veteran's club... and I'm sure you wouldn't believe me if I told you that we didn't know that it wasn't actually a stuffy old social club but more like a Las Vegas sports bar; multiple matches on the TVs and charming ladies in hot pants providing service with a smile. Oh well.

Despite our dishevelled look and growing pong making us unlikely customers of this restaurant, the girls welcomed us and chatted happily. A lovely young lady, Nicole, told us how passionately she feels about the homeless situation and gave us £5. She told us about a drop-in centre in town and a mixture of her charm and our guilt took over, making us divulge our true status. She was intrigued by the Trampface mission and asked if we'd like a photo with all of the girls. Of course, our inward, shy character meant that we took a little bit of arm twisting to be coerced!

Our quest to find the drop-in centre that Nicole had suggested took us back over the bridge and into town; it then had us stood in front of a window transfixed with the vision the other side of it. The large, clear, bay view window presented a woman rocking back and forth on a chair and singing into her e-cigarette. "This is some contrast to Hooters but I think we've found the drop-in centre my boy," Paul said. Our quest wasn't going to be fulfilled however, we rang the buzzer and after a brief exchange we were told that we would need prior referral from the council and couldn't just 'drop-in'. The lady pointed us in the direction of the Clarence Hotel who apparently, on occasion, offer free beds to those in need.

In passing the Motorpoint Arena we noticed an influx of people colourfully dressed and heading towards it. There was also a familiar looking Cymru Coaches bus, the miserable driver wasn't present but a cheerleader convention was obviously in full swing. Unbelievably, he had been heading to the same location where we had landed up. You can dismiss and drive away from Trampface but you can't hide from them.

We homed in on the bar quarter of Nottingham to chance our arm at begging, it had proved lucrative at times to hit these spots and we didn't exactly have enough knowledge of any other areas to try. With memories of Trackie Tom and the Navy Seal Team of begging from Cardiff, I decided to try a new approach. A lot of the bars were a standard portrayal of wannabe swank; smart chairs and tables outside, cordoned off by silver poles stretching out black fabric to create barriers. I patrolled the edge of them scanning for people sat outside and leaned over at intervals to say, "Hi, I am sleeping rough. Would you fancy buying my friend and I a drink or sparing some change?" I received tuts, scowls and complete silence... not a penny.

I returned to Paul and gave him a knowing look, he smirked and said, "Well, you can't turn into the Cardiff Olympic begging team overnight my boy," which lightened the mood. We were to receive some more cheer from a passing family seconds later. The mother had sent her young lad across with his little fist clenched. He shuffled closer to us with a wide-eyed look of uncertainty and gleefully opened his palm to reveal a pound coin that rolled off into our hat. We said, "Thank you young man," warmly which made him leap for joy before turning to run excitedly back to his family. We then shouted, "Thank you" towards his family which stopped his mother in her tracks. "Are you Welsh?" she asked. We confirmed that we were, thinking it was going to be an encounter of, "My granny is Welsh" or "I love going on holiday to Wales." Oh no. She then nudged her son in our direction and jokingly said, "Go and get our pound back boy, we don't give to immigrants." We all laughed and wished each other a good night. It was a great piece of humour to keep our spirits high.

A young girl with a compassionate face approached us and introduced herself as Devon. She sat down with us and chatted. She explained that her Dad was involved with a charity that offers support to ex-servicemen. After showing extreme concern for our well-being, she rang her Dad and told him about us. We spoke to him and he asked for our details. We explained that we'd rather not give them but take his instead. He gave us his contact details and implored us to reach out to him the next day. "Devon, we will ring him in the morning as we are sorted for tonight," I lied. Devon reluctantly left us and I felt humbled by her concern. Once we were on our own again Paul said, "Bless her. Just proves we must be starting to look really rough and pitiful."

Our quietly comfortable setting was about to be broken, by a brush with the law. From the darkness we were startled by a commanding voice bellowing towards us, "Right, you lads… you are not allowed to be here doing this." He had a defensive posture and it seemed like he was expecting us to react aggressively or bolt. When I replied, "We understand sir, we'll be on our way, no trouble." the police officer seemed surprised and calmed his manner and tone down to a more compassionate one. He then took a seat next to us and explained in depth the policy of Nottingham Council, "It's zero tolerance towards vagrancy lads, a status which you qualify for with your begging sign. Since Christmas there has been a major crackdown and the streets have been blitzed, I doubt you've seen many if any other beggars such has been the concerted efforts and success. Most cities issue a notice to leave the city for 24 hours but we go straight for the Section 35; leave the city immediately accompanied by a summons to appear in court."

This was serious, we were looking at being ordered to a court appearance without warning. This was something we hadn't at all prepared for.

We expressed shock at the harsh treatment meted out by Nottingham which was no doubt influenced by its dependency on high and mighty, demanding tourists. The officer conceded to some agreement but insisted they were following the law and simply enforcing it more efficiently than others. He continued, "Listen lads, considering your polite nature and attitude I'm not going to book you, my preferred intention is to offer you some advice if you'll take it?" We of course agreed. He rang the local homeless hotline and pleaded our case for assistance and accommodation but to no avail; nothing could be done until morning. It was pleasing however, to hear the system that they operate; if we told them where we intended to sleep rough they would check up on us sporadically through the night. A great gesture and worthy of anyone's respect. "Shouldn't be too hard to find us, just follow the noise of Tramp 2 snoring and the smell of piss," I told the officer.

The friendly officer gave us a rough sleeper's help card and showed us the route to the Clarence Hotel. While he still had his small, paper, tourist map out I asked him a question, "Hypothetically, if the hotel is full, what would that large cemetery over there be like for dark, covered corners?" He smiled in return and answered my speculative pointing at his map, "I'm sure it would be fine," with a wink. He demanded our personal details in exchange for not charging us so he could run a check that we weren't wanted or a danger to the public. We obliged and once our details flashed up on his device he looked up and said, "Hmmm were you both born in Swansea and Neath and are your nicknames 'Roundhead' and 'Westy'?" We shot each other a look of shock, tempered with a smirk and I replied, "No sir, we are commonly known as Tramp 1 and Tramp 2." The officer scoffed playfully and said, "Okay lads, if you say so. You boys take care and I hope you get to where you're going in life."

The route to the Clarence Hotel took us through the main square of the city. Here we noticed three very lively hobos jigging around to a stereo and drinking cheap, high strength lager. They seemed like our kind of guys and an opportunity not to be missed, so we bowled over. They didn't really seem like homeless men to me, more like working class men who wanted to drink with their mates but couldn't afford a pub. Plus they looked foreign and maybe the pub scene in the UK didn't suit them, or they didn't suit it.

They looked at us with suspicion as we approached and were clearly weighing us up. Initially they were apprehensive and didn't reply to our greeting, instead they conferred with each other in their native tongue. We persisted with our friendly tone and eventually they relaxed and offered us a can of lager. Result. It must have been our soothing, friendly, Welsh accents.

The lively group of three looked Eurasian so I was little surprised when they explained that they were from Poland; maybe based on my ignorant preconceptions that all Polish are like Paul the Pole from Trampface Swansea with his ghostly appearance. Tramp 2 and I had actually been to Poland a couple of years ago, a place called Wroclaw on a random last minute decision. I really couldn't use that as a reference on the appearance of Polish people though as I spent the whole three nights blind drunk. Speaking of 'Paul the Pole', we were about to experience a deja vu moment.

Malik spoke the best English of the three and adopted the role of leader and spokesman. He had strong, tanned features and a handsome, friendly face. He shook our hand and told us that he was currently a baker and 52 years old. The other two men were absolutely cuckoo and couldn't keep still, they were constantly jostling and jumping around. They were all from Krakow and Malik explained that he had arrived in England nine years ago and had sadly spent three of them homeless. The only thing we gleaned from the other two was that one was called Paul and they were retired police officers in their homeland. 'Paul the Pole II' spoke in a really high-pitched voice and told us, "We all work in the bakery now lads, we start at 4am but we love sitting out here drinking every night, it's our happy place where we can hang around together."

When asked, we explained our cover story and Malik expressed sorrow that he couldn't offer us a place to crash for the night. "I'm really sorry guys, you would be welcome, but I now have girlfriend. She is Romanian Gypsy woman and very crazy, even more crazy than Paul the policeman." We had a good laugh with the Polish guys and they seemed like genuinely nice people. We finished our free beers, shook hands, bumped fists and then set off into the night.

Several fast food outlets were still open but nearing closing time, so we decided to chance our arm in begging for some scraps. We entered Five Guys, BK, McDonalds x 2, Subway x 2 and met the same response in each place, "Sorry, but our hands are tied by head office and we are not permitted to give you any food." We pointed out that they were closing and the racks were still sporting wrapped food but still found no joy. The most we got was McDonalds offering to refill our water bottles. As we left Tramp 2 said to me, "I guess the manager of Cardiff BK that gave us all that food doesn't give a toss about head office. Legend."

Out of curiosity we had one last attempt at scoring some free food from a place that wouldn't normally have a head office; a Turkish kebab shop. After propositioning the thickly stubbled, rotund gent behind the counter we deduced that he was an avid Bob Marley fan. He stood smiling at us whilst shaking his head and singing, "No money no food... no money no fooooooood." Although a little annoyed we did have a chuckle about it whilst leaving. It didn't sooth our rumbling bellies though.

Embarrassment was to follow disappointment on entering the Clarence Hotel and enquiring about free accommodation for the homeless. The young girl behind the counter scoffed and patronisingly told us, "There is no free option here gentlemen, this is a hotel with some cheap offers for backpackers occasionally." Trudging back out into the cold I looked at Tramp 2 and said, "Looks like Nottingham War Cemetery is about to receive two more stiffs. Although I'm a bit concerned your snoring and our laughing at reading back the notes from today's events may wake the dead."

The eerie gates of the cemetery loomed ahead, and the orange glow of the street lamps soon gave way to the inky blackness of the graveyard beyond. Although we aren't men that scare easily, this was the first time either of us was going to spend the night sleeping in a freezing cold, pitch black cemetery; right amongst the old graves. We slipped through the wrought iron gates and my heart skipped a beat at the appearance of three young men. On closer inspection they seemed to be students smoking weed. We must have appeared more intimidating than them as they very quickly backed away and left. A perimeter sweep revealed that it was a very old cemetery with some headstones dating all the way back to the 1800s. Many were broken and had obviously been untended for decades. They had the look of the typical type you would see in the graveyard of a church in a classic horror movie. Mr Richard Birkin, 62, was about to become fortunate enough to receive two childish but friendly tramps to keep him company for the night.

We laid ourselves out right next to his tombstone and calmed each other from the shadows, casting ghostly visions in our minds, by sharing jokes from the day. We were also comforted by the belief that not many other idiots would be skulking around this creepy enclosure on a cold, dark night which would ensure a disturbance free night. Ghosts aside that was.

"Night night Hiker 1,"
"Night night, Hiker 2,"
"Night night Mr Birkin."

HITCHHIKE DAY 4

"Road to Nowhere"

First light brought with it a familiar scene, the Tramps pressed side by side, freezing and trying to share some warmth. Daybreak revealed a clear view of our position and it was quite a novelty being sat on the upside of the sloping graveyard; getting a panoramic view of the morning mist lifting above the tombstones to reveal a commanding view of the area. The long grass of the graveyard facilitated the collection of a heavy amount of morning dew and the moisture had engulfed us. My backpack was soaked and my sleeping bag around my head and face was also wet. Not a nice feeling when already shivering and trying to draw energy to start the day.

"Joonnoooowww, alright my boy?"
"Jooonnnnooowww, yeaaahhh, you my boy?"

Our childish ritual of addressing each other as "Jonnooww" in any written or spoken greeting had not gone away. Well, we *had* been doing it for around 15 years, so it was a hard habit to break. Although to this day, we still couldn't give anyone a single reason why we had started doing it.

Our morale was soon lifted by news of a radio interview and we were excited to receive a phone call from Badge and Claire, the morning show hosts that Paul and Ceri had won their wedding from. With the wedding just a few weeks away the station were keen to keep up with the progress of the Groom and Best Man. This was surely an unorthodox build up to a wedding, having the Groom sleeping rough and gallivanting around the country with strangers. I'm sure it made the whole event far easier to make appealing and catch the attention of listeners. We cleared our dry throats, put on our positive hats and had a humorous chat on air; although our location of a war cemetery was a little surprising to them. "You what," was the call of bewilderment from Claire.

We were relieved but also kind of disappointed that Mr Birkin's relatives had yet again failed to show up and tend to his grave. We bid farewell to our sleepover buddy and took comfort that someone had paused to think of him today and would forever remember his name from this adventure. Kitted up, we headed for the exit. In the daylight we realised that the cemetery was a lot bigger than we had realised the night before and our perimeter sweep had missed quite a few areas... including one we now saw sporting two tents. How the other half live hey!?

After three years of riding our Trampface luck, our bubble was sure to burst at some point, and today was set to be that day.

The town was heaving with a student crowd making their way to class and we decided to test their generosity and kindness. Some mobile begging was to be chanced and we took turns to walk through the students shaking a coffee cup and asking for "spare change". We were receiving some sympathetic looks but looks only which soon dried up when my iPhone 6 happened to drop out of my pocket to the floor. It was picked up and handed to me by a female student sporting a look saying, "Really?" I gave her a look of acknowledgment back, we laughed, and Paul said, "It's from the Job Centre, so we can keep track on all the high powered companies in need of our services."

The student rolled her eyes, pursed her lips and swung her hair as she spun around to walk off. Paul continued to talk to me, "No money and a look of scorn, we'll put that one down to experience shall we my boy?"

Back in the square we had a quick look around to see if Malik and the boys had made it into work and, satisfied they weren't still there, we moved into Wetherspoons for a coffee and to write the daily update. Paul checked the charity donation page and relayed to me that it was looking fairly neglected, "Time to pull on the heart strings my boy, we need to get this total rolling," he said with gusto. At the bottom of the update we wrote the following paragraph:

"We hope you are loving these updates as much as we love bringing them to you. However, we are feeling sad and unloved, over 12,000 people have read the last two updates yet our Just Giving page is sat at £350. We will keep pushing ourselves to entertain you and all we ask is for you to dig deep. As Poundman Dan would say... if you all give a pound, well we will be quids in.
Even Mr Birkin had a word about it with us this morning, "I can't understand it boys, why aren't your followers 'coffin' up?"

An old Royal Marine buddy of mine had seen our post about being in Nottingham and had hopped on a bus from a town 40 minutes away to come meet us for a catch up. 'Dits Dolby' lived up to his old nickname and we spent a good hour or so reminiscing over war stories and tales of high jinks. There was also a more serious side to the chat as Keith told us about his struggles with PTSD and depression since leaving the Marines. I'd had conversations online with Keith in the past about his dark days and mental battle but it was of course much rawer to hear them when sat next to him. He told us about his journey and praised the positive impact volunteers had had on him. Keith was an up close and personal example of the reason we need to keep supporting the charities.

Our chat was interrupted by a man in his fifties, smartly dressed and accompanied by an expensive tweed jacket on the back of his chair. It was now 10am and the gentleman had been sat at a table next to us happily slugging pints of lager on his own. He noticed my SSAFA military charity t-shirt and asked me if we worked for them. We told him the Trampface story and he told us his story... at great length. It was plainly obvious that John, a retired RAF officer, greatly missed service life and everything that came with it. He now spent his days at a loss about what to do with himself and expressed the desire to get involved with a military charity to not only help others but also for his own well-being. It was sad to witness a proud, smart man who seemed to be rapidly losing his direction in life.

Daily update posted, we left the sanctuary of the warm, coffee refill station and braced ourselves for some time in the cold with a thumb out. After the previous day's success at the Shell station we thought we'd try our luck at another one. The location we'd identified was on a very busy road with vehicles regularly pulling in and out, but the attitude of the motorists appeared frosty. Time was getting on and we were keeping our spirits up by saying, "We'll get something soon my boy, just remember how well we've done up until now." For three long, freezing, agonising hours we alternated between holding the sign and a thumb out whilst the other Tramp rewarmed his hands. "I think there's more chance of our fingers falling off than getting a lift here my boy," I said through chattering lips.

Tramp 2 agreed and then became noticeably downbeat, "Insult to injury my boy, here come the cops." A police patrol car stared intently at us as it drifted past before turning around to approach us. The hostile nature of Nottingham and its officials towards our 'type' was again plain to see. We were told in no uncertain terms to move along and were told rather patronisingly, "You are welcome to leave the city boys, anytime you want, but I'm afraid you'll have to pay for the transport." I became patronising in return and said, "Actually we aren't doing anything illegal." I was promptly told that I don't make the rules on these subjects and if *they* decided we were vagrants then that's what we were.

Cold, annoyed and feeling sorry for ourselves we trudged back into the town centre. "Screw them, there was no need for that attitude, we weren't causing any trouble," Paul grumbled. I agreed, and he continued, "Let's go do some more begging in town to see if we can acquire lunch. If those lot turn up again we'll just leg it." We needed something to occupy us as the few hours of being stood around had numbed our brains as well as our extremities. Back in the same spot as the night before we looked around and realised the area was pretty quiet. It took ten minutes before we were approached by two council wardens who grunted at us to clear off. We really weren't in the mood for a couple of bully boys in bright yellow jackets so I replied, "Why don't *you* clear off," with a menacing look. It was followed by Paul rising to stand his 6'4" frame up in front of them.

The wardens assessed us for a minute and could see we weren't playing ball or scared of them. Paul raised his eyebrows at them and they started to back away, accepting that we weren't going to comply easily. Then, like a couple of snivelling weasels, they grinned at us whilst they radioed for assistance from some PCSOs (Police Community Support Officers). Tramp 2 called them a couple of cowardly shithouses and I couldn't help but snigger. Now at a safe distance they called us a couple of "gypo sheep shaggers". Paul took a few steps towards them and as they backed off he said, "We shag them, you eat them. Now do yourself a favour and get lost you pathetic rats."

The afternoon was slipping away from us but we decided to hang around, we wanted the situation to be escalated by the fuzz before we resolved to leave. Our sorry, unhappy faces paid off when £4 was dropped into our hat just before we caught sight of two PCSOs bearing down on us. I turned to Paul and said, "They are dressed in cumbersome kit, and by the looks of them, definitely not fans of physical exercise. Even with our back packs on we are beating these two in a foot race… easy." Tramp 2 agreed, and we grabbed our bags and walked away briskly. As predicted the officers declined to follow us.

Time was getting on and I had become completely fed up with Nottingham and its attitude towards us. Both of us were agitated and frustrated, we must have looked like a couple of forlorn figures as we paced away from the city centre. An impromptu meeting around our small paper map saw us weighing up our options. We agreed that it might be better to try an area on the outskirts of the area with a higher volume of cars likely to be heading towards the M1 and major arterial routes. Surely anything had to offer more hope than what we'd experienced in the town centre. The wind had picked up and the lack of food to warm our blood was making us shiver. Just around the corner we saw a shining light, a family-owned chip shop, and we did not hesitate to enter to use our begging money for a warm bag of chips. Our menu choice came to £5.50 but we managed to convince the owners into giving us a discount and the recently acquired £4 begging money was handed over.

They say that misery likes company and the term was wholly appropriate for our next attempt at thumbing a lift. In the way that our previous misery was accompanied by another dose of it. Another disaster, with not a single bit of notice paid towards us… apart from the all too familiar sight and sound of the local police. The men marching toward us were different officers to last time, but the crackle from their radios told us that we were marked men and word had been put out about us. Our names and appearance were becoming well known and the officer in front of us sighed back into his radio, "Yep, definitely them." The officer adopted a strict approach and we were delivered a final warning, "Next time we catch you in the act of vagrancy you will be recipients of a Section 35 and a court summons."

Resigned to defeat we dropped our heads and walked in the direction of the M1, kicking the ground and cursing our aggressors. A quick map check confirmed it was a ten mile walk in total from our start point at the Shell garage to our current position of purgatory. I was seething at the dressing down and threats by the police. Yes, we were clearly a couple of Tramps but unless they caught us in the act of begging how could they realistically pin vagrancy on us… it's such a grey area and vague activity to pin on someone. Most cities had little tolerance for beggars and tramps, which I can understand why, based on certain experiences, but in Nottingham the officials and law enforcers were ruthless and persistent; committed hardliners. We deduced that our chances of hitching a lift here were non-existent. The only option standing out was pressing on by foot to the nearest service station; at least we could get a coffee inside and hold a mini parliament about the way forward. It was still a fair trek so we attempted a last ditch effort to plead for a ride. We flagged down some public transport and asked the bus driver if he could give us a lift for free, but even bus drivers apparently now hated us.

At around 8pm we caught the sight and sound of Trowell services up ahead. A coin was flipped to decide our fate… heads for north, tails for south. With little confidence or conviction, we had one last go at begging outside the entrance in the dark. Needless to say it was a waste of time and we both cursed our luck. The moon was up in the clear night sky and the temperature was dropping quicker than our options had. "Let's call it a night shall we my boy?" Paul said with defeat. Feeling depressed we slipped through the lorry park, casting some very envious glances at the truckers cosied up in their cabs for the night, and headed towards a treeline skirting some farmer's fields.

The fields were isolated from the service area and any human traffic, but were exposed to the wind and rain. The ground on the side we were stood was boggy and unsuitable so we hopped the fence. The other side was still damp but had longer grass making it slightly more cushioned. We were exhausted, cold and fed up, so it would have to do.

We both laid down and quietly reflected on our day's failures and the tough time we'd received from the police. Throughout all of our Trampface adventures, including rough nights in the Calais Jungle, we'd always remained positive. Today we felt dark and dejected with the belief that we had let ourselves and the Trampface mission down. Writing tomorrow's defeated update was not being relished at this point. We made a promise under the bright moon to take it on the chin and leave it behind come the morning; accept a hard lesson and make better decisions for the remainder of the week. It was foolish to always rely on confidence, luck and charm.

Our low mood wasn't going to stop our rhythmic and joyous night-time ritual under a stunningly bright moon though. After a long sigh we persisted with it in an upbeat fashion whilst reverting to our now treasured, original nicknames:

"Night night Tramp 1,"
"Night night, Tramp Twwwoooooooo."
"Get fucked Nottingham."

The day had undoubtedly been an absolute stinker, probably the worst in the history of Trampface… but little did we know that tomorrow was going to redress the balance, by delivering an absolute belter!

HITCHHIKE DAY 5

"Batman Bill and the Penthouse Suite"

Jokes and laughter through croaky voices and groggy heads, was how Day 5 started. It was probably the coldest night so far thanks to the clear sky, but we had promised to get a grip of our doldrums and hit the day with positivity from the start. "At least we are not laying on a pile of needless and human excrement," Paul said. He then assertively pointed at the services through the trees and added, "Coffee and a ride north waiting for us in there my boy."

We delivered the update in a somewhat less enthusiastic manner than we'd become accustomed to, due to the shocker in Nottingham, but we were buoyed by the immediate messages of morale-boosting support. A quick check of the charity donation page revealed that our current total fund had trebled overnight. Wow, Paul's idea to plead for more donations had worked magnificently. A strong coffee had also helped to better our mood. "I guess old Mr Birkin asking why they weren't coffin up did the trick," Paul said with a smile.
"Good old boy is Mr Birkin my boy. I'm hell bent on getting away from here today," was my reply.

We ended the update with this:
We do read the messages of support from you on there and they go a long way to keeping us smiling so please continue. You are legends. Please keep sharing, donating and taking a leaf from our begging techniques to get friends and family onboard the Trampface juggernaut. Toot toot.
Daily begging total £4
Lots of cold thumbing love,
Hiker 1 and Hiker 2 (Not from Nottingham County Council).

Renewed vigour was searing through our veins and we dominated the entrance and exit to Trowell services; capitalising on the choke point with friendly smiles on our grubby faces. We were resolute on getting away from here this morning, no matter what we had to do.

An elderly man dressed in smart clothes, a bit like your grandpa would wear to the country pub on a Sunday afternoon, approached us. He expressed sorrow that he couldn't give us a lift but wanted something from us instead… our precious time and attention. Les launched into a 20-minute tale about his life and regaled us with stories about his time in the jungles of Malaya. He was an affable man just out to pick up his morning papers, but his presence had not helped us at all in our quest for conveyance north. Who knows how many potential lifts had passed us by whilst we were otherwise engaged with Les.

Moments after Les had said goodbye we noticed a smartly dressed businessman looking at us intently. He was leaving the building and still on the other side of the glass exit doors. "I noticed him looking at us curiously on his way in my boy," Paul whispered. The man drew level with us and then turned to speak, "I'm going to Leeds if that's any good lads?" We looked at each other with glee and replied, "We would love a day out in Leeds mate." Tramp 1&2 were back in business and as we hopped into an executive-looking car I said, "Goodbye Nottingham, you certainly won't be missed."

Jason introduced himself and told us that he was from Eastbourne and married with two children, he was on his way to head office in Leeds. We thanked him for offering us a lift and asked, "Do you mind us asking why you picked us up, just out of curiosity?" He laughed and said, "Yea I'm a serial killer, gotta keep the run going." Paul replied, "So are we, what are the chances? Shall we team up?" and we all had a giggle.

Jason continued, "To be honest lads I saw and heard you talking to that old gent and just thought you seemed like really sound guys. I have plenty of room and it's always nice to have some company on these long rides."

We chatted happily and relayed the Trampface mission to him, in return he told us that his son would soon be heading to Uganda for a charity project and that he was very proud of him and his selfless ways. "He'd be really intrigued by you guys, he's a real outdoor enthusiast and Bear Grylls fan." Paul perked up as he is a massive fan of the survivalist adventurer and has all his books and productions. Sat in the back, I smiled at the Bear Grylls mention... I had been in contact with his production team at the outset of this year's Trampface and had even been sent something whilst Tramp 2 was asleep next to me in Cardiff. This exchange would remain my little secret for now...

Jason probably feared that our toxic hobo skin would soon start melting into his expensive leather seats and so offered to drop us off on the outskirts of the town centre. We quickly hopped out at a red light and thanked Jason for his generosity.
"Right then my boy, what do two lively Tramps do with themselves in the historic city of Leeds?"

City of Leeds, Northern England

Leeds is in the county of West Yorkshire and has a population of nearly 800,000 people. Its motto is *"For King and the Law"* and it is commonly referred to as *"The Capital of the North".* It has four universities and is regarded as the biggest financial centre outside of London. It is home to the oldest surviving film in existence, *Roundhay Garden Scene* (1888) and saw the invention of soda water in 1767. Its name translates to 'People of the fast-flowing river'. This derives from old Brythonic (related to Welsh) and the meaning of it follows the similar theme of Welsh places such as Swansea – Abertawe in Welsh, meaning 'Settlement at the mouth of the Tawe (river)'. It is also said that "Leeds" came from the Welsh word 'lloed', simply meaning "a place".

Some interesting facts about Leeds are:

- Hippo bones dating back over 100,000 years old were found in the city and now reside in the City Museum.

- Leeds University has its own Quidditch team, the Harry Potter inspired game is adapted to be played on foot however.
- The 2nd ever Ryder Cup (and first in Europe) was held in Leeds in 1929.
- Back in 1884, Michael Marks opened up a penny bazaar stall in Leeds Kirkgate Market. A decade later, he enlisted the help of Tom Spencer to grow the business and they went from strength-to-strength. Soon after, M&S moved to a permanent spot just around the corner in the Market and the rest, as they say, is history.
- In 1975 Leeds United FC (occasionally called 'Dirty Leeds') became the first team to introduce replica shirts for fans to purchase; so you can thank them and your football crazy children for being penniless every season.
- Leeds resident James Henry Atkinson invented the 'mouse trap' and the patent was bought by the Proctor Brothers; the design is still sold today.

The list of famous 'Loiners' is not that distinguished but no doubt recognisable to some: **Mel B** from the Spice Girls, The **Brownlee Brothers** Triathlete champions, **Leigh Francis** (Keith Lemon) the TV personality and **Malcolm McDowell** the actor, to name but a few.

Leeds also has a very impressive city hall, especially when viewed from close up or above, but more on that particular building later…

It cannot be underestimated how much morale can be gotten from just a few small acts of grace when sleeping rough for a few days. A coffee and chat with Jason had left us in an optimistic state of mind and the arrival in a new city, holding so much potential adventure, had us buzzing with excitement. There was a definite spring in our step as we paced towards the action of the town centre and we had a footloose feel about us, "It's like the first day of a holiday my boy," Paul beamed. Despite being extremely worn down and tired, a new place offering new opportunities was as good as a rest and we were eager to get stuck in.

A begging plan needed to be formulated but first we had to answer a call of nature. Now being in the thick of the town centre hubbub we noticed a Yates' bar and ducked in to use their toilet. Stood waiting for Paul, I noticed the girl behind the bar singing cheerfully to herself and as Paul approached I called across to her, "I know it says on the sign outside that it's karaoke tonight, but has it started already?" The girl smiled and replied, "Yea, what are you singing boys?"
"Stick us down for Phil Collins *Another Day in Paradise."* I replied playfully.

We set up by the window with a pint of lager to observe the main thoroughfare of this busy city street and to pre-identify any good spots. Paul pointed out a suitable position, "Just over there my boy, next to the bus stop and at a T junction of food outlets, shops and benches. We could squeeze in there and guilt the throngs of people into parting with their cash. They will be coming from all angles and there will also be people waiting around for a bus. They will have plenty of time to mull over our misery and react." We agreed it was a cracking spot but from experience also realised we would soon likely be set upon by some form of officials. If their policy was anything like Nottingham's, then our positive outlook would soon be tested.

Business was slow for 20 minutes, but we kept the faith as it was early and we had a great spot. It wasn't too much longer before we received a couple of interactions with the people of Yorkshire and momentum soon started to grow. An interesting and different point to note was that most of our benefactors here were teenagers. Many stopped to talk or drop a few pennies in our hat and it was really great to see. We also received a Big Mac to share from a lad that called himself 'Ginger Mac'. Mac was from Scotland and I thought he was wearing a Glasgow Rangers top, the team from his home

city, but on closer inspection I could see it was a Chelsea one. I asked Mac about it, expecting that he had been given it, rather than from being an avid fan and he replied, "Yer mate, Chelsea through and through me, best team in the world. I have been a devoted fan since I was a wee 'un."
"Naturally, what with West London being right on your doorstep," I said, sarcastically.
Another teenager approached us and donated two fresh, warm cheeseburgers. This spot next to McDonalds was turning out to be a right touch.

Our cover story had now been forced into a change due to our present location; it was unlikely that two Welsh men would be in Leeds when citing their goal as being to reach London. To any inquisitive/nosey individuals we were now heading for the dockyards and building sites of Scotland! Our story was soon about to be tested. We had managed around 40 minutes without any intervention from the authorities which was pretty good considering the prime spot we had occupied. However, the shadow of a formally dressed Environmental Enforcement Officer was soon cast over the tramps and the man stood looking down at us. The role of the Environmental Enforcement Officer is to try and limit the incidences of dog fouling, littering and anti-social behaviour within the County Borough. We couldn't immediately work out his intentions or mood so we remained cagey; after all we *would* fall under the 'anti-social behaviour' bracket. Nottingham still lingered very much in our thoughts as he prepared to speak.

"So what's the story boys, make a good impression and I'll show some leniency?" was his opening gambit. He was dark haired and a little unkempt in the grooming department, the exercise and healthy eating one too by the looks of his jowls and muffin top. He seemed to me like he had a slight inferiority complex; maybe from a rough time as a youngster… this made me a little bit guilty about my initial assessment of him. His manner definitely displayed a level of wanting to assert power in his position and that was maybe why he had chosen this career. He was grilling us about our cover story and trying to catch us out, although he didn't seem to be leaning towards moving us on.

Our routine of explaining our cover story was now well rehearsed and we promptly answered any questions with confidence. His tone remained calm and he seemed as though he was enjoying talking to us and wanted to remain on friendly terms. His advice was for us to go and visit the local Royal British Legion around the corner and request help. The officer's relaxed demeanour then suddenly became very agitated and we saw him become fixated on two ladies approaching us wearing Leeds 'Meet and Greet' uniforms. He became fidgety and light on his feet, like a sprinter about to slip into the blocks… and straight back out of them. He started backing away and just before turning to take off he parted with a warning, "This woman is gonna absolutely torture you boys, sorry but you're on your own."

Then he was away as quick as a flash with not so much as a glance back at us.

We laughed and wondered what could be so awful about the pale, fragile old lady approaching us with her young apprentice in tow. We'd soon find out. Patricia and Hannah were both dressed in black overcoats and bowler hats with badges attached to them. They were employees of a friendly local scheme to give advice to visitors in the city centre. They approached with warm smiles and arms held abreast offering a warm hug. We eagerly accepted the hugs and they probably lasted a little longer than the ladies had anticipated or wanted! However, I soon withdrew after receiving a good lungful of Patricia's traditional old lady perfume.

Patricia was in her 60s and a very sweet, gentle woman with the desire to help others. She soon took her revenge on our lengthy, pong-ridden embrace by engaging in a lengthy, unbreakable, one-way conversation. She then made the unfortunate error of revealing her spinster status to us and as soon as we identified a pause we pounced. We turned the tide and launched into some extremely rigorous and risqué flirting. Patricia noticeably became very uncomfortable with our boisterous, good-humoured advances and started to back away. This only succeeded in us upping the ante and teasing her even more. They were now reeling backwards and as they made their excuses to leave, I turned my attention to Hannah and said, "You got off lightly, we hadn't even started on you," whilst laughing cheekily. Hannah understood the repartee and gave us a playful look of disapproval in return.

"I don't think they'll be back in a hurry my boy," Paul said with a smirk.

Very soon after our shy, shell-shocked ladies had departed we received four steaming hot cartons of tea; this led us to be concerned about the literacy levels of the people up north… today's sign clearly stated "Will accept food, COFFEE, water and hugs." Two timid teenage boys offered us their packed lunch and we, of course, refused. The boys became persistent and stubbornly told us that they wouldn't leave until we took it; a very touching gesture. A frail old man carrying a cane hobbled towards us, he looked weathered beyond his years and offered us four~~,~~ hot~~,~~ Gregg's pasties. His hands were shaking terribly and from his brief exchange with us I garnered the impression that he himself had spent some time in our position. We laughed when he dropped a fistful of sugar sachets into our hands, like they were gold dust, but in reality the sight of him lowering down to offer us this kind gesture really got to me. An overwhelming feeling of humility washed over me and I felt completely humbled by this elderly man displaying so much concern for us. I knew nothing of him, or his story, but had a moment of quiet in my own thoughts and wished the world possessed more men like him.

The familiar shadow of our Environmental Officer once again darkened our patch. He now had a colleague at his side and I got the impression he had run off to find him. I had visions of him tugging on the other officer's shirt saying, "Come, come quick... come and meet these two Welsh Marines I found begging," doing so like a kid that had just found a dead animal down the park. The grilling resumed but he had clearly been away to do some research as the questions became a lot more specific to my military credentials and background. Maybe a little doubt had crept in.

He soon admitted that he had been on the phone to his best mate, a Sergeant in the Royal Marines. Suddenly, I felt like I was stood in front of the Sgt Major and being interrogated about my actions; "Where's your kit, why didn't you get a travel warrant, what unit were you in, don't you have normal clothes to wear instead of a mix of old military stuff?" We did laugh when he asked if our red hoodies were Royal Marines issue! I batted away all of his questions of course, I wasn't the Walter Mitty he'd been sent to catch out. Knowing the sceptical nature and distrust of other people that most Royal Marines possess, I knew his mate would've instantly questioned our credibility. He'd have lined him up with all the questions to try and catch me out... if only he knew that I was a serving Sergeant myself.

The grilling soon calmed down and Paul received a handshake containing a £10 note. A very noble gesture, considering he should've been handing out a warning or worse. They wished us well and headed off to find some dog walkers to fine for fouling. Turns out the officer was a hypocrite, he'd tortured us more than sweet Patricia had. We concurred that he wasn't our type however, so the Trampface flirting tactic was kept under wraps. We had endured two exhausting, verbal onslaughts so far but the best/worst was about to come, and it would have us in uncontrollable fits of laughter.

Ladies and Gentleman, please allow me to introduce to you... the one and only Batman Bill, Leeds's very own premier vigilante...

Bill, a man in his 50s, was balding, had square spectacles and was wearing Dr Martens. From his mouth containing merely two teeth (one top, one bottom), we were for the next 40 minutes subjected to the lightning paced, unbelievably enthusiastic but far-fetched stories of the saviour of the North. To make this less painful for you than it was for us, but just as hilarious, here is a brief overview of his achievements and accolades to date:

"I spent 10 years in the army lads but now I'm signed off as disabled. In 1991 I single-handedly led the research team deep into Iraq to find Saddam's depleted uranium. I'm the only one from the team still alive now and I watch my back, the government want me dead because I know too much." He threw a glance over each shoulder for good measure after telling us this.

Bill then rolled up his trouser leg to show a nasty chunk of flesh missing from his lower limb, "I recently had my leg chewed by two Pitbulls lads, I had come to the rescue of a domestic abuse victim and they set the dogs on me. The Pitbull owner was due in court yesterday but he's still in hospital, recovering from the seeing to I gave him."

Bill had the manner of a man I'm sure you've all come across at some point or at least could relate to. He had a very average stature and features but told incredibly fanciful stories you just knew weren't true. But he told them in such an enthusiastic way that you knew he actually believed them himself. He was now in full flow and wasn't going to miss the opportunity of a captive audience with no immediate reason to leave:

"I was an electrician in the army but then I was singled out to become a German linguist because I had such a knack for languages. They threw me in halfway through a course and I became fully fluent in less than six weeks." Bill lauded.
I sarcastically replied, "Wunderbar Bill."

"I loved my time in the army and because I was so decorated, I was allowed to keep my three rifles and revolver after I left. Unfortunately, I had to use them the other day though, to shoot a rapist. Shot him four times. I thought I might have been in trouble but the Chief Constable gave me a pat on the back instead. I had to wait in the cells while they went through some formalities and that, before I got my pat on the back, but I still got special treatment in there; a cup of tea and a book of my choice."
We were both already staring and shaking our heads at each other and cracking up. Any sane person would've stopped and asked us why we were laughing at them, but not Bill, Bill cracked on regardless.

"So I chose Murray Walker's Autobiography. Read it complete in 24 hours. As soon as I finished it I went back to the start and began reading it again. The police returned my rifles and revolver but gave me a warning about my profile. They said I had to stop being known by the nickname 'The Executioner'. I explained that if that is what people choose to call me then I can't do much about it. But I promised that I would stop telling people that it is my dream job."

After some counter questions from us, we established that his revolver was actually a .77 air gun. No doubt the rifles were pellet guns of some sort also.

Batman Bill had us absolutely enthralled with his tales and the more he told, the more we laughed. He had the perfect mix of telling ridiculous tales but not overegging them or getting *too* excited. The stories were the perfect level of 'matter of fact' delivered with a straight face, occasionally breaking into animation. It was the serious look he gave us after each one that had us cracking up the most, like he was being completely straight down the line with us and waiting for us to agree in a serious way. Unfortunately, our story time was about to come to an end, but Bill still had time to leave us with a couple of crackers:

"I'm going to have to go boys, I'm on the number 52 bus and it's already gone past three times. Anyway, all the best lads. You don't seem like most of the others I meet… last summer I was walking my pooch through the cemetery and I caught a tramp making love to a dog. Ooof, couldn't look my pooch in the eye for a week."

We were in absolute stitches, doubled over on the cold pavement with tears running down our faces. "Auf Wiedersehen Bill, take care, Gotham needs you more than Grantham."

We finally recovered from our aching ribs courtesy of Bill and soon had more company, unfortunately the unwanted kind. An unimpressed PCSO arrived on scene and wasted no time in laying the law down. He was in his 50s, skinny and had a creepy grey goatee. He took a firm approach and told us, "Come on you pair, move it. This is your notice to move on before I escalate matters. I'm bound by council policy and our current main effort is to eradicate people like you." We both snapped our heads at him and he clearly got the message that it was for his use of words. He looked like he'd been caught with his hands in the cookie jar and immediately started back peddling. After some 'Errring' he gave us a grovelling apology for using the term "Eradicate people like you". I didn't buy his apology, they were clearly his thoughts, but he had just phrased them in an unpleasant way which we had picked up on and which may get him in trouble.

Accepting that our run of fortune in this spot was at an end we begrudgingly stood up to leave; I was more disgruntled by the warden's manner than the actual act of having to leave our spot. We'd had a very successful hour or so next to the bus stop and we were thankful for the experience. At around the same time that we were giving the PCSO a last look of disapproval we were approached by a beetroot faced man who introduced himself as Jeff. He was an ex RAF rank who was keen to take us for a pint. 'Alcy Jeff' asked us if we'd like to join him for a drink and a chat in the warm and I replied, "Would love to mate, we've not had a pint in weeks, thanks." Tramp 2 threw me a cheeky grin.

Jeff was mumbling and slurring away whilst leading us to the nearest pub and I'd hardly had time to look up before realising we were back in Yates'. I was adjusting my eyes to the dimness inside and before Jeff could order some beers, the singing barmaid cheerfully greeted us, "Alright lads, back for the karaoke are you… same again is it?" and immediately started pouring the pints. Alcy Jeff looked at us with utter confusion, trying to fathom what was going on and we just shrugged our shoulders, acting as if we didn't know either.

Jeff was clearly an alcoholic, albeit a functioning one with a wife and grown up kids. He had his military pension which allowed him to honour his family commitments and spend afternoons in the pub every day. It is clearly hard for a lot of guys to leave the forces family, routine and environment and find something else to occupy their life with. Jeff told us that he just didn't have the motivation that he had before and sees his only outlet from boredom being on the end of a bar each day. He explained that he would meet a regular group of locals who would also drink all afternoon and then head home for dinner. They all had partners at home and were not homeless alcoholics. "I love meeting and talking to new people too lads, thank you for joining me it's been really great," was Jeff's sad departing line.

We tracked down the local Royal British Legion, as advised by our friendly Enforcement officer, and were gutted to learn that it was simply an office, not a dusty old bar like the one in Swansea! We introduced ourselves to Jenny and Suze and they made us a coffee while Graham gave us the lowdown on their work. Graham was now blind, and he displayed a trait I have found in most visually impaired people I've met; a great sense of humour which included mocking himself freely. The gang had been expecting us after a tip off from the Enforcement officers. We told them the Trampface story, posed for a picture and headed back out onto the streets.

A few people around town had alerted us to a drop in centre called 'The Crypt'. It seemed intriguing, so we took a wander around the city to get our bearings in an attempt to locate it. In the large main square we caught sight of two homeless men sat on a concrete ledge. We asked if we could join them and one of them looked us up and down before preparing his sedated mouth to speak. He was dressed in a baggy grey tracksuit which didn't suit his tubby, middle-aged appearance. He had a rolled up woolly hat on but I could make out his ginger/grey hair and beard beneath it. The man replied in an Irish accent, "Aye lads, take a seat. I'm Dermot, from Tipperary aye."

Dermot had the presence of a man with an inflated level of self-importance and entitlement. He was even arrogantly swaggering in his seated position whilst dragging long pulls of cider from a plastic flagon. He was surrounded by empty cans of strong, cheap cider and still had a carrier bag full of more; obviously flush and able to acquire things easily as he didn't hesitate in offering us a can. Feeling it would be rude to decline this ice breaker we gladly accepted. The pressurised 'Psssshhhttt' of my can opening was challenged in the air by another distinctive sound, the second man's iPhone ringing. The younger, gaunter man then made a sharp exit, telling Dermot he would see him later.

The cold concrete ledge was making me fidget and I decided to distract myself and take out the notebook that I use for jotting down occurrences for the daily updates. It was really surprising how much stuff we actually forgot about until reading the notes back the next day, considering it had all just happened only the day before. Such was the worn-down condition we were in; our minds just didn't function as well as normal. Many times we would sit and read the notes and say out loud, "Ahhhh yea, I forgot about that/him/her." The notebook had become a vital tool and we would force ourselves to use it regularly, even when we just wanted to keep our hands warm in our pockets.

Dermot immediately zoomed in on me and my jotting, "What the hell is that, a police notebook? What are ya doing?" he snapped. I told him to calm down and explained that if I was a copper taking notes on him, I'd hardly whip out the pencil and pad in front of him, would I? Dermot became more abrasive and wary of us and asked where we were from. Paul said, "Port Talbot," and Dermot asked if we knew the O'Briens; a notorious family in the area according to Tramp 2. Dermot asked our names and said, "Aye, I'll ask around about you's pair." We asked Dermot the way to The Crypt and he quickly pointed out the direction and how to get there. I asked him if we would get any trouble being a couple of new faces on the scene, expecting a routine reply about not worrying. In contrast to my expectation, he slowly and purposefully nodded his head in confirmation that we would probably get some trouble, and then added, "Especially with that notebook Boyo."

A gaunt looking boy/girl couple were striding across the square in our direction and Dermot immediately made a noise that awarded them the same status as unwelcome neighbours dropping by. They seemed quite lively and keen to chat but told us that they weren't too fond of their current residence, "Why have you Welsh lads ended up here? Leeds is the worst place in the UK to be homeless, it's a shithole and full of ignorant, selfish people. We hate it." Was the statement from the male of the pair.
"How long have you been here?" I asked.
"Four years," was the response I got, so I challenged them and said, "Four years, well it can't be that bad then can it? In fairness we have found the people to be very friendly and kind."

The pair mumbled something and then started bragging about being clean from heroin for a few weeks and that they were no longer shoplifting. A deathly silence descended once they had realised we weren't really interested in talking to them and they soon awkwardly shuffled off. Once they had departed Dermot said, "If they are clean and not on the rob, then I'm the mighty King of Ireland."

Next it was Dermot's turn to leave and he gave us a grunt of a goodbye, akin to Royalty dismissing their subjects. He picked up his remaining bag of cans and slithered away across the square. Left all alone we decided to conduct an experiment whilst still in possession of our nearly full cans of cider. "Let's put the begging hat out and sit here openly swigging our cans of cider, see what reaction we get?"
The reaction was complete avoidance and half an hour later we had zero pennies to show for our efforts.

The Crypt drop-in centre was down a set of dark, narrow steps and boasted two securely locked doors. We rang the buzzer and a balding man in his 30s shouted through the glass, "What do you want?" We explained that we were homeless and after help. He was uncompromisingly blunt in his response, "Can't help you sorry lads, there's a mobile soup kitchen setting up shortly, just around the corner." He waved us away in the direction of the imminent food drop, "Try them."

There was a decent sized group waiting for the soup kitchen and we soon mixed in with them and made some friends. Our accents attracted some questions, but they were born from friendly curiosity rather than a challenge. The atmosphere was jovial and well mannered. Once the mobile food van was set up we received a surprising meal comprising of a solitary banana and slice of cake. Slightly miffed, but grateful, we wolfed down the sweet offerings, although it had the effect of making me hungrier than I'd thought I was. Luckily, we then witnessed the unorthodox delivery of the main meal arriving after the dessert. Our eyes were wide and our mouths drooling at the hot pasta, chicken and potato in front of us. A couple of minutes of silence ensued whilst we devoured the meal and washed it down with hot coffee. The volunteers were their usual happy, relaxed and interactive selves, although one man in his 20s did subject us to some heavy scrutinising of our background story.

Still without any idea where we were going to sleep we decided to wander the town some more and possibly find a spot for some late-night begging. We were in good spirits from our busy day and wanted to ride the wave while we could. It was dark by the time we passed the impressive Leeds Town Hall and we noticed it was under renovation and covered in high scaffolding, which was also draped in tarpaulin. "Now that is interesting my boy… and potentially a new challenge for the tramps to attempt."

Town was getting pretty quiet so we slouched near some late-night fast food places and laid out the begging hat. We chatted for around 40 minutes without any disruption until three British Pakistani lads stopped for a chat and gave us a tray of chicken, chips and a burrito. We were about to tuck in when out of nowhere jumped a fellow starving hobo who started enquiring about our fresh food. He then started guilt tripping us about being on his patch and doing him out of a meal; the guilt trip worked and he was soon the happy recipient of a burrito. The rest of the food was divvied up between us and not long after we had finished licking our lips we were approached with more offers of food. A friendly young man and woman appeared with a flask and some wrapped up ham rolls. We were still hungry and gladly accepted the treat. Burrito Boy had scarpered, it seemed like he wasn't that fussed about his 'patch' after all.

The couple bearing food were not from any official charity. They were partners who just deployed to the streets on occasion to search out people in need and give them some support. "Now that you've taken some food and coffee, can we ask where you are sleeping tonight lads?" the young lady asked. We said that we weren't sure. As much as these people seemed trustworthy we really didn't want many people to know of our movements and plans. After all, we ourselves were trustworthy people but not telling the whole truth to people whilst on the streets. Paul gave them something, "We were maybe thinking about Holbeck Cemetery as we've had some luck with solace in those type of places in the past." The girl took a step backwards and gasped, "Guys, do not go there to sleep, in fact avoid it at all costs at any time of the day. It is a notoriously well-known and feared drug abuse area and red-light district."

Paul joked back, "Sweet, how much do you think a couple of handsome Welshmen could earn in one night?" She stared back with a look of confusion about how serious we were.

We held a discussion about our plans and decided that after the poor effort in Nottingham we owed it to ourselves and the mission to try something risky and make amends. The goal was to make an audacious attempt to scale the Town Hall. If successful, we could claim a penthouse suite at the very top, providing a bird's eye view of the city, for free! It wasn't going to be at all straightforward and we would need to conduct some reconnaissance in order to weigh up the full scale of the task. It didn't quite have the same status as a routine building site in Bristol.

We set up an observation post opposite the well-lit building in the doorway of a bank and assessed any hurdles that we'd face. We opened a can of lager to share and help with some courage if/when the decision was made to scale the Town Hall. The first deterrent to look for was any roaming security; we couldn't see a static one but needed to be patient. Another factor to consider was the need to give ourselves some sort of boost up to reach the first floor of scaffolding, as any ladders had naturally been stowed away… you know, to stop trespassers gaining easy access. This boost up to gain initial entry would need to be conducted swiftly; the area was brightly illuminated with orange floodlights and in direct view of the busy road next to it. The adjacent road had a set of traffic lights which were in line with the scaffold entry point. This caused a backlog of vehicles every so often, complete with the wandering, curious eyes of the stationary drivers. Our timing to dart across the road and break in would need to be executed with military precision.

There was a huge factor playing on my mind which increased the chances of grave consequences if we got caught. It was the fact that there had been a terrorist attack in Brussels *that day* and this meant the authorities would be on high alert. We were talking about breaking the perimeter of a high-profile, historic government building and our actions would carry a high risk of arrest, and even the accusation of terrorism. The danger and risk levels were as high as the prestigious structure we were gawping up at, but we felt we owed something to the followers that had donated and supported us. Our resolve was stiffened by being mindful of our epic fail in Nottingham. And the truth was that we really fancied hobnobbing with the Town Hall hierarchy and dignitaries, high up above the city.

During a break in the stream of town traffic we seized the opportunity to dart across the road; heading directly for a corner, which housed a gap in the boards above. Paul, being 6'4", gave me the first boost up but I found some difficulty getting through. A loud whack of the boards echoed off the old building and I winced at the disturbance. As I had thrust myself upwards, my backpack had wedged me in the aperture, which was designed for a human *without* luggage. I managed to wriggle through and then told Paul to throw his backpack up to avoid the same drama. With Tramp 2 now clean fatigue he kicked off the wall and I grabbed hold of him by his arms; he then hauled himself up and through the gap. We were in.

The structure had been breached but we were still unsure if anyone had seen or heard us enter and we moved forward with trepidation. Now that we were in the main holding of the scaffolding there would be ladders to take us up each floor. Caution was still to be exercised as we couldn't be sure whether there would be internal security or even some other Tramps with the same idea as us. Each time we climbed a ladder one of us would poke our head up over the lip of the next platform and scan for any movement. I slowly raised my head up over the lip of a floor and my heart skipped as light from below cast shadows across the wooden boards. It took an age for my eyes to adjust to the dark and I felt vulnerable, like a wobbling head at the perfect height to be booted by a lurking soul. It was quite eerie and exciting at the same time, creeping and peering through the dusty, dark, temporary corridors.

Our footsteps were light but still causing creaking and a good amount of dust to rain down below. The tarpaulin sides were a welcome feature allowing us to move unseen from the street below. Eventually, we reached the top floor of the scaffolding which sat astride the roof of the Town Hall. Our penthouse was covered from above by the roof of the building and from the sides by the tarpaulin and outer wall. With the wooden boards and sculpted stone decorations of the building around us, it felt like we were residing in the Royal suite of an Edwardian Castle. Tramp 2 grinned at me like a Cheshire cat and I let out an excited laugh. We were brimming with pride at our accomplishment of sneaking up to this most lofty, spacious and privileged set of accommodation. I walked a little further into the darkness and called back to Paul, "Great view of the sky across the city, I wonder if this is where they keep Bill's Bat Sign."

We were flush with space and had cover from the elements on all sides. The floor was hard so we utilised some cardboard from the building site and laid down to rest and reflect on an epic day. What a turnaround it had been from the previous 24 hours. It had been the perfect tonic for the recent difficulties faced and we relaxed with a strong feeling of satisfaction. Total begging money received from the day: £65.25. Tiredness was soaking in and our eyes were soon closing on a fantastically rewarding and majestic sight across the city.

"Night night Hiker 1,"
"Night night, Hiker 2,"
"Gute Nacht Batman Bill"

HITCHHIKE DAY 6

"Anyone Going South?"

I woke up absolutely bursting for a pee. I scrambled out of my sleeping bag and ran around in different directions, desperately trying to work out a solution to my bulging bladder. "Just do it off the side," Tramp 2 shouted whilst giggling. "I can't do that mun," I called back through shallow, pained breaths. Moments later I realised I had no choice, it was either piss myself or just go off the edge. To make it a little more respectable I moved to an edge that had a skip full of rubble below. There I stood, a reputable man in his 30s relieving himself from the roof of Leeds Town Hall, in daylight and above the busy morning commuters.

"Disgusting my boy, wait until I tell our followers about this. The all so noble Tramp 1 thinking he's above everyone else so much, that he can get up in the morning and rain piss down on them."

Our spirits were high and we were both laughing as we carefully climbed down the scaffolding, scanning for any arriving workers or security as we went. Tramp 2 continued his verbal ribbing of me, "You spend one night in the prestige of the Town Hall and think you are King Arthur. God help if you ever get into politics my boy." One after another we dropped down through the ground level opening, dusted ourselves down and walked off briskly to blend in with the morning rush of workers. Safe in the knowledge that we were now in the clear, we started revelling in our cheeky night in the penthouse suite and were excited to include it in our update.

The time was a little after 7am and the day was young; begging was to be chanced to try and take advantage of people's early morning light-headedness. We crouched down and huddled against a cold shop wall and after around a minute were walked down by a skinny, scruffy man in a white cap and tracksuit. The lad wasted no time in engaging in the now painfully familiar ritual of telling us we were on his patch. We were in a good mood but I really didn't have time for this bullshit anymore. I told him it was a free country and we had got here first then turned my head away to ignore him. It was apparent that this had provoked him, he became livid and started ranting at us, "You fuckers are part-time beggars, frauds. Don't you know there's a street beggars code and you are both disrespecting it. You don't look in need of help and you're not even from around here. Wankers like you ruin the chances of locals like me getting the help I need."

I was feeling threatened and exasperated so I challenged him back, "You what mate, you're a local? You've got a Scottish accent you knob. I didn't realise we'd been teleported to Dundee overnight."
Jock boy mumbled and stammered back, "Yea I'm a Scot but I've been here two years," and then kicked our begging hat. Tramp 2, knowing that I'd developed a short fuse towards anyone defacing our begging equipment, let out a low "Ohhhhhhhhh" sound and put his head in his hands.

I stood up in a rage and gave our annoying 'local' friend a warning, "I couldn't give a toss how long you've been here or where you're from mush, but I suggest you make yourself scarce. I suggest you do it as quick as you can, I really do." After five sleepless nights and a lot of bullshit, our patience was starting to wear thin with these rude, entitled idiots.

We possessed enough loose change for a coffee and we were just one sticker shy of scoring a free one by completing our loyalty card. Paul came up with a simple solution for us to redeem the free one; well we thought it was simple right up until he tried to explain it to the young lady behind the counter.
"If I order two coffees, can I pay for one with cash and then remove the sticker from one to complete my card to redeem the second?" Tramp 2 asked.
Server girl, "What?"

Tramp 2, "If you give me the second coffee in lieu of money, I can use the one I paid for to complete our loyalty card?"
Sever girl, "Do you want one coffee or two? You have to pay for both."
Paul tried to explain it in a different way several more times and the girl just stood there with her mouth and eyes wide open with no idea what he was asking. Paul turned to me and said, "Flipping heck, am I talking Swahili here my boy?"
This seemingly simple request had turned into a saga, so Paul changed tact, "Okay, you clearly don't understand my basic question. Right, can I have a coffee please, just one?"
The girl brought him the coffee at which point he then quickly removed the sticker, put it on his loyalty card to complete the set and then handed it over, "Can I have a coffee please?" The girl suddenly had a hallelujah moment and exclaimed, "Ahhhhh," before bringing us another coffee.

Our friend Simon (the copper that had loaned us the stab vests for Calais) had alerted a facebook page called 'Bullshire Police' about our rough treatment in Nottingham. The page was a spoof account, managed and followed by serving and former police officers to make fun of their organisation, people and situations. We had received a bit of banter from Bullshire and had taunted them back, to which they had put a call out for any officers to try and hunt us down. A small, friendly game of cat and mouse. In light of this we had started taking pictures of any police patrols we saw and posting them online with a taunt about being one step ahead. This morning's picture was a riot van parked metres away from us.

We mapped a route to a petrol station, approximately three miles out of town, to try and hitch a ride from. This would take us through the dodgy, no-go area that we had considered bedding down in the night before. The area, even in daylight, seemed to fit the description given to us by the friendly volunteers last night. We knew the moment we had crossed the threshold into Holbeck as the dynamic and surroundings instantly changed; it was like an episode of Ross

Kemp on gangs. Tramp 1&2, being keen sightseers, decided to take in a full tour, this came complete with shitty nappies on the street, graffiti advising "Never Work" and metal bars on house windows, doors and anything that could be entered through. It was striking to look down a row of terraced houses and see full length metal gates covering the front doors. We also witnessed a comical domestic argument in the street over an electric heater with one leg; it was getting pretty nasty. The area had a steady stream of 18-year-old pram pushers; completing their look by smoking ~~a~~ cigarette and dressed in baggy pyjamas and Ugg boots.

We paused outside the police station to take a picture of the fugitives on the run from the Bullshire detectives and rub their noses in it, Trampface 2… Bullshire Nil. A fruitless hour was endured at the petrol station and we were beginning to get that sinking feeling again. Our luck changed when a dark-skinned man in a lorry started smiling and waving his arms at us and pointing towards the main road; the international sign for, "Where are you going?" I guessed. Ravi the Romanian then said, "Where you go guys, I help yes?"
We replied, "South mate, Birmingham? Bristol? Cardiff even?" and were delighted when Ravi excitedly shouted, "Yes Cardiff, yes."

What an absolute stroke of luck, a trip all the way back to Cardiff. Or so we thought…

Ravi spoke very little fluent English but he was animated and funny, so we were hopeful it was going to be a good trip. We were motoring along at a decent speed and soon hit the motorway; neither of us was familiar with these parts and weren't really paying attention to our surroundings. That was until the horror of a motorway sign was pointed out to me by Tramp 2, "Oh shit my boy, look at that sign. THE NORTH. We are going to Carlisle not Cardiff." My heart sank with the realisation that Paul was right, we were going the wrong way.

What a disaster, Ravi's poor English had led to a misunderstanding and we were tearing away towards the Scottish border. This would've been great four days ago, but we had made the decision to start hitching south or face a mammoth train fare home on completion of Day 7 if we kept going up.

"Ravi mate, you are going to have to drop us at the nearest services please mate," was our request after explaining our predicament. He was laughing his head off and trying to convince us that we needed to improve our Romanian in future. Once at the services Ravi jumped out to see us off and was still hysterical with giggles. The sight of him laughing and making fun of us just made us laugh back at him, which made him laugh even more. Three lard heads stood in a carpark laughing at each other. It's all fun and games until you end up 300 miles from home, heading in the wrong direction.

Desperately needing to make headway towards Wales, we pushed straight across to occupy a spot by the main entrance to the amenities. Our haste in scrounging for a lift bore fruit almost immediately. A man called Justin came up to us and said, "Hi lads, I can take you as far as the Manchester area if that is any good?" We eagerly accepted and jumped into his van. Justin looked like a grafter, he was well built, had worn hands and a robust demeanour. We learned that he was a plasterer and undertakes the renovation of houses for the Canopy Housing Project. They make houses habitable for the homeless community of the north and are funded by the National Lottery. Justin explained that he had endured a spell of unemployment during the late 1980s during the spell of Thatcherism and he'd faced a struggle to fight his way out of it. He told us that his son is now his apprentice so that he can guide him through a vulnerable time in his life and show him the value of hard work. Justin made us laugh when he said that he'd also hitchhiked as a young man and had enjoyed many adventures but added, "My success did dwindle as I started to get older though lads; I could no longer rely on my baby-faced good looks."

Justin dropped us at a service station near Manchester and we thanked him for his kindness and conversation. Time and light were fading fast so we needed to get straight into begging for another lift; believe me, we were not two guys that people would voluntarily approach in the dark! This forced us into employing a new tactic. I stood with our sign in view of passing people and Paul started vocally campaigning for our cause by asking, "Going South?"

The first person to walk past us was a woman heading towards her car. Paul propositioned her and her response was to keep looking forward and simply shout, "North," in a gruff, uncompromising voice. Undeterred, Paul turned his attention to a smartly dressed man in his 20s following up behind. After a pause the man said, "Ummm yea, well, Chester?" We accepted his reluctant offer and I feel he only agreed because we had put him on the spot and his politeness not to say no took over. The back seat of his hatchback was cleared of papers and DVDs and we were soon on our way again. Chris told us about his work in the dockyards of Hull and his personal passion as a fixed wing flying enthusiast. We told him he was only the second person we had badgered for a lift and that the first woman had simply shouted, "North" at us before walking off. He gave us a perplexed look and said, "That's funny, we were on the southbound services, there is literally no exit to go north. What a cowardly woman using that as an excuse instead of just saying no."

Chris dropped us at the near-deserted Warrington-Lymm services, where we braced ourselves for a night stranded in the cold. Of course, we would still have a go at hitching first but at least we had made progress thus far and had chipped away at the trek south. Sadly, for three long hours we tried everything but to no avail: the fuel area, truck stop, McDonalds drive through and even the toilets for a chat over a pee. Seems as though the men of the north don't appreciate being disturbed whilst in full flow!

Sensing our despair and hopelessness a one-armed trucker named Paddy brought us a couple of coffees of his own accord and stopped for a chat. He apologised for not being able to give us a lift, citing the rules about him being classed as a disabled truck driver and so not being permitted to carry passengers. We weren't sure of the truth or circumstance behind that but enjoyed his company anyway. We had a photo with him and wished him well on his journey.

At 11:30pm we decided that enough was enough and the deserted service station wasn't going to deliver us any form of transit salvation. We called it a day and started looking around for a set of bushes to crawl into for a few hours. The side lane of McDonalds had a view into their loading bay at the rear and we found some old advertising hoardings; they would give a nice layer of protection between us and the damp floor. The forecast for the night was 3 degrees and the chance of rain. For a reason I can't understand we hadn't brought any kind of overhead cover on this trip, not a poncho or even a thin sheet. This absence of protection made the potential appearance of rain a veritable disaster.

Our position of refuge was a narrow, shallow ditch with a tree line one side and earthy bank the other. We'd slept side by side on every night of our three Trampface missions so far but tonight we'd have to sleep lengthways, head to head. We rested our heads on our backpacks and prayed that the rain would stay away. "One more night after this my boy."
"Would've been a couple more if Romanian Ravi had had his way."

"Night night Hiker 1,"
"Night night, Hiker 2,
"Night night Bullshire."

HITCHHIKE DAY 7

"Awaking to Rain and Five Minutes of Fame"

The pitter patter of raindrops was the sound and vibration I awoke to in a ditch just outside a service station. The temperature was cold but that wasn't going to stop us from rapidly exiting our sleeping bags to get going. I quickly stowed all my kit away and put my jacket on to take the brunt of the rain starting to fall. It was still very early but I was glad the rain hadn't come earlier and drenched us as we slept. Tramp 2 was good to go and so we made a rush for the services.

Passing truckers were giving us curious looks as we dragged our decrepit looking arses out from beneath the trees and drifted past the parked-up trucks. Maybe they were concerned we were trying to rob from their trucks or stow away in them; we certainly looked shifty enough. Our bones were as cold as Mr Birkin's so we made our way to the coffee shop for a hot beverage and to write the daily update. We thanked everyone for the donations and messages so far which always meant so much to us whether morale was high or low.

There was only one night left of this Trampface mission and we had been warned off about a possible ITV Wales interview on our final morning. It was just a possibility at the moment but it was developing and if was to go ahead it would be conducted back in Cardiff. If it looked like it was on the cards we'd agreed that we would want to be as close to Cardiff as possible, or we'd miss out on a fantastic opportunity to promote the Trampface mission and the charity. This meant getting a real shift on towards the South as soon as we could. The problem was that the people of Warrington-Lymme Services didn't share our same sense of urgency.

Another miserable five hours passed with us standing sheepishly with our sign and kindly asking passers-by "South?" The week had borne overwhelming generosity and kindness from strangers but this morning was showing us the ignorant and cold-hearted side of people. Some looked at us in disgust, some didn't even offer a polite "No" or "Sorry I can't", and *all* refused to help us. It seemed as though Warrington-Lymme Service Station is a statistician's dream; out of the hundreds of people going through there, not a single one was going south… apparently.

Feeling that helpless, deflated emotion in our stomachs once again we psyched ourselves up and decided we would have to do something different to change our situation; even if that meant making a tough call. The only option we could think of was moving to another set of services and hope that it was busier and had a better layout for us to approach people. Knutsford Services seemed a bigger and busier place and we were convinced we'd have better luck there. The problem was that it was seven miles away, it was raining, and those seven miles were as the crow flies; it would be a different prospect on foot when following meandering paths. Whilst mulling it over, we realised that today was a memorable day for us both personally. On this day 13 years ago a young, skinny, ambitious lad from a council estate, called Westy, stepped foot through the gates of the Commando Training Centre, Royal Marines. At the same time his best friend, Paul O'Dwyer, was dug-in on the Kuwait/Iraq border awaiting the imminent order to advance. With this fresh in our minds we steeled our nerve, hardened our resolve and set off on foot with renewed vigour.

The seven miles or so to Knutsford took us through country lanes and dirt tracks, which we ran down, and private farmer's fields which had us crawling through hedgerows and avoiding the tractor patrol. We evaded trouble and arrived just short of the services, muddy and a little sodden from sweat and drizzle. I hopped over a fence into the courtyard of a compound and Tramp 2 landed next to me as I was looking around to suss it out. It turned out to be a police enclosure post, doh. The uncompromising and startled face of a police sergeant appeared and immediately questioned where we had come from. We brushed past him at a canter and I called back, "Bullshire Sarge, don't worry, we've been good boys and we'll send them your love." He looked at a loss at what to do and just watched us trot away.

On entering the services we immediately noted it was a much better prospect, it was larger and absolutely heaving with people. The entrance also looked far more suitable for us to perch ourselves next to. Tramp 2 had gone to the toilet and considering our recent brush with the law I became concerned when he hadn't returned after a lot longer time than it should normally take. I was then even more alarmed when he did appear, smiling away with a young man in tow, also beaming with happiness. I was about to ask what was going on when Tramp 2 spoke first, "Sorted my boy, follow on." The young man smiled and gestured that it was Okay to follow. "What the f…."

I followed Paul and his new happy friend to a battered old Ford Transit van and as we hopped into the front I was still in the dark about what the hell was going on, or had *gone* on. "Right, someone explain what the heck is going on," I demanded.

They both laughed and Paul began, "I was in the toilet washing my hands when Arran here tapped me on the shoulder and asked me if I wanted a lift. I looked at him confused and said that I did, but how on earth did he know so. He then pointed out that our cardboard hitching sign saying 'South' was attached to the rear of my backpack and visible through the elastic straps. I told him that there were two of us and that you smelled worse than me but he was still keen to take us. I gave him a rundown of the Trampface story and that's why we took a while returning."

Amazing. Only Tramp 2 could get a lift hitchhiking without even asking for one, in the men's toilet! Brilliant turn of events!

Arran was from Stoke and until recently had been an apprentice mechanic at the Bentley Cars manufacturing plant. A brief appetite for the bad boy lifestyle, coupled with a taste for vodka, had temporarily led him astray. He was open and honest about his mistakes and laughed them off as a learning experience. With his apprenticeship lost, he now ran his own carpet cleaning business and maintained a passion for collecting and restoring old cars. We had a quick selfie after he dropped us off at another service station where we aimed to follow up our previous southbound services success (try saying that after an afternoon in Yates' with Alcy Jeff).

Stood braced for another potentially protracted thumbing session we opted to keep the momentum going and threw enthusiasm into our requests for a lift. We saw a pale looking man in a cap walking towards us and I tentatively asked, “South?” he very calmly raised a finger, suggesting he would be back in a minute. He did indeed arrive back after a minute and asked what our intended destination was. “Anywhere further south,” we answered and he said, “I’m going all the way to the coast, so just let me know where you would like to jump out.” I sensed a Scottish accent, tinged with a hint of continental Europe which made me slightly apprehensive after our recent tuck up by Ravi the laughing Romanian.

Adam was Polish but had settled in Scotland with his family some time ago. He was now a freelance courier with his own vehicle. He divulged his routine explaining that people would tender out a job for a package to be delivered and the couriers would then bid for it. The first bid to be accepted would get the job. They were often last minute, urgent deliveries where he would pick up the package from source and usually travel a long distance to drop it off personally. He said that most of the jobs were a fair trek and tonight’s one was all the way to Brighton on the south coast. This would see him sleep in the van before heading back the next day or hopefully getting another delivery coming north. It was good money but lots of mind-numbing hours driving, so he was glad of a bit of company. He made us laugh when he told us that he has black, window shaped stickers on the side panels of his van, to make it look like a Caravelle and avoid paying extra tolls. “Those extra tolls for commercial vans really add up lads.”

Adam told us tales of hitchhiking around Europe as a young man and that it was easy and carefree back then. "Everyone was doing it and people would have no problems picking you up," he told us. He also amused us with the backstory about his compulsory military service in Poland and according to their system he could still be called up at any time if the country deemed it necessary.
"Although it wouldn't be very exciting as I would be called up as a postman, meaning that I'd likely be the one delivering the dreaded notices to all the other poor conscripts that they had been summoned."

Our hearts once again skipped a beat at the sight of an unwelcome motorway sign. Adam had taken the exit onto the M6 toll road; meaning we were now heading south east, towards London. This was totally the wrong direction for us. After some Trampface pouting and charm, he kindly offered to go out of his way and drop us at the M42 services. We asked him if we had put him out and he politely replied, "Not at all lads, I have hours to reach Brighton and am well ahead of schedule." What a gentleman.

Despite a slight detour we were still full of optimism on the back of two consecutive quick pick-ups. With the five hours today and a whole afternoon and evening wasted yesterday at Warrington-Lymme now a distant memory, we were about to strike gold again. In the dark outside Hopwood Services, we saw that the place was absolutely heaving with Bank Holiday travellers; this was good in that they were numerous but could also mean that they were stressed and frustrated. Firstly, we received the tantalising offer of a lift to the M4 close to Wales and we were elated as we followed an ex-Navy man to his vehicle. Unfortunately, just short of his wagon he suddenly turned around and delivered a hammer blow to our guts, "Ohh shit, sorry lads. I've just remembered, I'm in the wrong van for this, I've only got one spare seat in this one." I tried to hide my utter despair but I'm sure he could sense my disappointment as I grumbled, "Umm no probs, thanks anyway." Paul cracked a joke and said, “Have you actually got a big minibus but just caught a sniff of us and decided there’s no way you are having two umming tramps in your wagon?”

It was a joke but there was no doubt that we were definitely starting to smell pretty bad. Back in the entrance we stood waiting for another offer. Out of the darkness came the voice of a real saviour, “You’re not going to mug me if I give you a lift are you lads?” was the half joking question aimed at us. Following these words we paced off with a short, dark-haired man in his twenties. The car we arrived at was just like the first one we had hitched a lift in on Day 1 with Steve; a silver hatchback. We just hoped this one had a healthy alternator and/or breakdown cover.

Ben was very laid back and talkative but also exuded a larger than life character and carefree attitude in general. He explained that he had had good reason for his opening line towards us, “I recently lived in Texas for 18 months lads, I got carjacked not long before moving back from there. Bastards took my Mustang, phone and wallet.”
Elated to be finally heading towards Wales, Ben told us that his parents were from Port Talbot which led to a chat with Paul about the area and families. Bizarrely he announced that he had lived near Warrington-Lymme Services for two years, which prompted me to say, “Two years in Warrington-Lymme, we can definitely relate to that.” Ben was a good guy and we enjoyed chatting with him, he told us that he’d recently worked in USA in recruitment for the oil and gas industry. A recent downturn in the industry had provoked him to move into IT. We swapped numbers as he dropped us off.

We had received an exciting phone call a little earlier explaining that the possible ITV Wales interview had materialised into an agreed appointment. This had affected our travel plans due to it being scheduled for the next morning in Cardiff. We felt it was the right decision to spend the night in Cardiff in order to be certain we would make the interview; the exposure for Trampface would be fantastic. The key decision meant we would have our final night to once again explore Cardiff and try something new…

Our options were these: to go and beg for cash one last time before finding a spot to rest, or once again approach the Huggard Homeless Centre and enquire about sanctuary for the night. We were already registered from our visit on Day 1 when we were denied a place so all we would need to do is pitch up and throw our names in the hat. Confidence was high after enjoying a string of good luck throughout the day. We of course felt it might be wrong to accept shelter but on the other hand we had also agreed at the start of this project to try and experience new things. We had slept rough on every single night of all three Trampface ventures so far so another night in a bush would be nothing new. If we were accepted for a night in a shelter we could report on the process, atmosphere and goings-on in such a mish mash of people thrown together. We agreed that if the unlikely circumstance arose of us looking like we'd get a space before others then we would turn it down flat and walk away. We were positive about this attempt and buzzing with expectancy again, Huggard Centre here we come. "I wonder if we'll bump into any familiar faces from Day 1?" Paul mused.

"This is Trampface my boy, it's nailed on," I quipped.

On our arrival at the imposing locked gates we saw a plethora of other sodden, desperate, shelter seekers. "Doesn't look positive for the Tramps my boy." Ziev, an Israeli pensioner waddled over to us to chat, thinking that he recognised us from before. I couldn't remember meeting him but he seemed amicable enough so we made small talk. Ziev soon moved on to his story and he appeared very down and depressed, he elaborated on his predicament with tear-filled eyes, "I had been receiving my UK pension and support as normal. I am a British citizen with a passport which was authorised from my father's heritage here. I had left the UK for a year and on my return I had been stripped of all financial and housing support, leaving me homeless and desperate. The Huggard Centre has been amazing with assistance in my legal battle to win back my rights and all I want is a roof over my head to call home and some help to get back on my feet. The drop-in centre staff are great but I feel very vulnerable in there, I am old and not able to protect myself; the police attend several times a day to deal with violence and it is very scary for me."

According to Ziev, two people had overdosed from alcohol and drugs there this week and were taken to hospital; the word was that they had died. He told us that he doesn't smoke, drink or take drugs and he didn't appear under the influence. He seemed like a genuine guy although we didn't have the knowledge to verify his situation with the government. If true, it is a shocking state of affairs that a British citizen could be left penniless without support, never mind the fact that he was a pensioner. This poor vulnerable man was destitute in his retirement years and tragically jostling for a space on the floor of a homeless shelter.

Waiting patiently I noticed a rain lashed umbrella approaching us and from underneath it poked a familiar, friendly face. "Hey guys, you are back. Did you miss me? It's great to see you again." Julian from Mongolia/Essex had arrived and brightened up the night. He even remembered our names and said he had been looking for us around the city. His week hadn't been so good though, clearly as he was now stood outside the Huggard in the rain. He had no problem being open with us and launched straight into explaining his situation, "Lads, I've been at it again. I just can't control my expenses, as soon as I get any money I gamble it away. I got paid and it was all gone that same night. Ten years lads, ten years I've been like this, constantly fighting myself but losing every time. I can't go on, I have to get help and put a stop to it. The centre has booked me in with a councillor in two weeks' time and I really hope they can help me."

Julian had an extremely humorous and endearing manner and made us giggle with his short fast sentences, fired out in that direct, blunt way that foreigners sometimes do in English. He was still clutching his four-season sleeping bag, fearing another night on the streets if there was no room at the inn. I was surprised he hadn't pawned it in but I guess there isn't much demand for a homeless man's second-hand sleeping bag. Julian passionately told us that we should command priority at the centre because we are former military, but we told him that our policy was to wait until all people waiting had been accommodated. Only then if there was any room left would we accept it. "We can fend for ourselves much better than most people and especially this vulnerable group stood next to us here."

It was unlikely that we would be anywhere near the front of the queue, we were from out of town and the staff weren't stupid, they could see we were healthy, aware, sober (ish) and able to look after ourselves. I did hope we didn't somehow fluke it to the front though as it would've been very awkward. Julian had been referred directly by a charity so he was confident of securing a place. The first cut came and left about five of us still stood out in the rain; Julian had made the list and we were delighted for him. He was a good guy and deserved some help and comfort. He shook our hands warmly and said, "I will see you soon guys, we will get you in tonight." As he passed a staff member he got his attention and said, "You see these two guys here, they are my friends and military men, they need priority, please get them in tonight." It was very touching to witness, bless him.

For another 30 minutes we stood stock still in the rain watching the inside door through the gates for any movement. We'd been hopeful of a space but that hope was diminishing with each passing minute. Tired and sodden we stood in silence dreaming of a warm, dry sleeping bag, this was in contrast to our lively, gung-ho attitude on our visit on Day 1. Our journey over the week had taken its toll on us. The five outcasts left outside all looked around at each other and we were sharing some sheepish looks of, "Oh well," and feeling sorry for ourselves. Suddenly the door opened and the staff man appeared. The looks between us now became anxious ones over which of us would get picked, if any at all, it may just be a final word to say they were full.

Three names were called and all of our fellow 'survivors' shuffled forward in glee, then we heard, "Paul, Lee… the military boys." My blood rushed with elation at our names being read out, we were in! We followed the group with eager anticipation and entered the reception area of an annexed building around the corner. The other three were led off in a different direction and we found ourselves in front of a reception 'kiosk' window. The two ladies behind the counter gave us a warm welcome and explained the rules and procedure, "You will receive a sleeping bag and roll mat for the night which you will place in that tub over there in the morning before you leave. Breakfast and coffee is until 8am and then you will have to leave. You seem like nice guys but unfortunately it is every man for himself in here and you will have to find a floor space in amongst the others in there. It's pretty full tonight lads so good luck."

This seemed a little more daunting than the comfortable, peaceful night sleep we had imagined. We were being thrown into a room full of addicts who probably all knew each other and had already established a pecking order. Two fresh-faced new boys were really going to test the dynamic of the order. We were big enough to look after ourselves but not whilst lying down in a sleeping bag in the dark against an unexpected attack. We made some small talk with the girls whilst they readied our sleeping kit and they asked about our background. They seemed sad and confused about why we had ended up on the streets and showed compassion towards us.

They buzzed the door to unlock it and no sooner had the latch clicked, it was forced open and two men thrust their heads out. They started to size us up; a bit like the small, curious dinosaur in Jurassic Park. The two men looked threatening and uncompromising and definitely like they were in charge of proceedings in the melee going on behind them. Glancing past them I could see a very large hall/room with lots of people moving around and a few already sparked out on the floor. Considering they hadn't been in there very long it was already in a mess. I was not relishing this one bit. The two men became aggressive towards us and one of them pointed at Paul's camouflage bottoms and shouted, "Ew don't need the cops in here tonight to impose my curfew now do you? We've got the British Army mun."

I think that due to a mixture of our quiet, polite manner and the potential friction that two new faces in a full room was going to cause, the staff closed the door to find an alternative. I guess they may have seen us as having the potential to push back against the challenge of the aggressors, unlike others, and that it may end up coming to blows. "Would you lads prefer a side office just down the corridor to yourselves, you really don't seem the type to cause trouble or start roaming around the place, so we'd be happy to put you on the floor in there?" Once again I succumbed to an overwhelming feeling of humility and humbly collected my black bag containing a clean fresh pillow, sleeping bag and roll mat. We enquired about our friend Julian and were told that he was inside but across the courtyard.

Sarah guided us to our boudoir, all smiles, and apologised for the light not working. Paul replied, "We'll be out for the count in seconds hopefully and it saves us having to look at each other." We smiled at each other at this most simple luxury that was now causing exhilaration in us and then removed our clothes and socks for the first time in a week!

"Holy shit!"

I hadn't noticed any pong emanating from us during the week, apart from an earthly damp smell from my jacket, but the smell that now hit us was absolutely disgusting. It was pungent, raw and suffocating in its thickness. I was startled at how it had instantly clogged up the whole room with such an overpowering stench. I said to Paul, "Our trainers and socks are the main source my boy, we're gonna have to leave them outside." Paul interjected, "They may get stolen."

I argued that it was a risk worth taking and would be a funny story if they actually were, but he insisted we keep them inside. I really hoped my tiredness would knock me out sharpish… but if not, the smell probably would anyway.

There was a knock at the door and Sarah poked her head in, and immediately reared backwards in response to the smell. I felt extremely embarrassed and tried to apologise but she clearly wanted to say her piece and disappear as quickly as possible. Sarah presented a polite request to us, "Lads, there's been a bit of a mix up and we have one more person to accommodate over here. I don't want to put him in the main action room, so would you mind having one more in here with you?" We of course said it was no problem and were pleasantly surprised at the sight of the new addition, for it was a familiar face. It was Julian from Mongolia/Essex and he smiled as we shouted, "Oi oi… here he is."

Sarah legged it and the smile on Julian's face from our friendly reunion quickly disappeared. He started to wretch and put one hand over his mouth and used the other to try and waft the stinking air away from him. "Jesus lads, has something died in here?" He flung the door open and then started ripping into us. Our embarrassment gave way to his funny nature and the comedy he was providing us with his animated words and reactions. We were sat up on the floor in stitches of laughter at his performance. "Don't you shower? Put those shoes outside, you can bin the socks… Sports Direct has good sale on Donnay." With this he flung our shoes and socks straight through the door and they bounced off the opposite wall in different directions. "I can't handle this; can you smell it guys? Believe me it's really bad."

Our laughter was starting to calm down when Julian reached into his bag to retrieve something, it was a strongly scented aftershave and he started rigorously spraying our bare feet with it. We were looking at each other crippled with laughter. He was spraying like a man possessed and after about two minutes he handed the spray to us and with a tone of defeat, he said, "Please guys, as much as you like... I get from pound shop, please keep using," and then he let out a sigh of exhaustion. We were done, we were absolutely howling. There we were lying on the floor of a homeless shelter with a Mongolian gambling addict spraying our feet with a manly musk aftershave. Truly a one off, completely unparalleled.

For the next hour we ignored our fatigue and desire to sleep in exchange for Julian's company. We chatted and joked and he revelled in showing us videos of pranks on YouTube on his phone. He once again displayed his pride in his Mongolian warrior heritage by trying to show us the same video of Genghis Khan from Day 1. This was even after I'd said, "You've already shown it to us you bonehead."

Julian finally decided it was time for sleep with his 6am rise in mind. He had to report for work in his role as a security guard for Securitas. We shared a smile and had a content feeling as we signed off for our last night as a pair of hitchhiking hobos and this year's Trampface adventure:

"Night night Hiker 1,"
"Night night, Hiker 2,"
"Night night Julian."

"Jesus guys, I can still smell your feet..."

HITCHHIKE DAY 8

"The Chequered Flag"

Sleep was warm, safe and dry but slightly interrupted when at 05:45 Julian's alarm sounded. He apologised for having to wake us and got up to slip into his uniform for work. We jokingly wolf whistled at him and told him how smart and handsome he looked. We were like a group of old friends, talking and joking in a personal, open and well-intentioned manner. Julian then brought the mood down a little and I felt sad when he bowed his head and said, "OK, don't anymore lads, I'm embarrassed by this and having to be in this situation." We reassured him that he has what it takes to get through it and wished him a good day. Julian smiled and said, "You too guys, I will see you later."

"You can *bet* on it mate," I said with a snigger and we all laughed before Julian replied, "Haha very funny," with a wink and a thumbs up.

I was sad to see Julian go, and of course I knew that we wouldn't see him later on or likely ever again. I genuinely wished him all the best for-the future. I felt a friendly attachment to Julian and had the urge to just swap details in order to take him under my wing in the future. Maybe I could help him, maybe not but I wished this friendly, honest guy all the best. Maybe the fact that he shared the same first name as my late father led to an unconscious connection for me. Although, my father was not a fan of the name and only his close family used it. To his friends, workmates and new acquaintances he introduced himself by his middle name, Steve (Stephen).

Sarah came to check on us and explained coffee would be on until 8am, at which time everyone must leave. She paused whilst turning around and gave our scattered trainers and socks a funny look. Paul shouted, "It's a Mongolian tradition, you throw your footwear at the wall outside before sleeping to keep away the demons." She giggled and left us to it. We had a prior arrangement to speak with Claire Scott, one of the breakfast show presenters from the Wave radio station, so we decided to skip coffee and get going. It was just after 7am when we handed our kit back, said thank you and slipped away towards the town centre. The phone call from Claire and Phil came whilst we were walking and we had a morale boosting chat with them. They were keeping tabs on us because Paul had of course been stitched up with, I mean happily won, the free wedding and it was only a couple of weeks away.

The ITV Wales interview was still a few hours away so we wanted to get a good start on delivering the final update to get it posted, allowing us to relax on our journey home. We settled for a coffee in Wetherspoons (free refills) near the window and basked in the spring sunshine penetrating through. In the update we praised the Huggard Centre and their staff for the service they provide and the kindness and support they had shown us. We posted that if any of them ever read about our time there we sincerely hoped they wouldn't be annoyed. We always promise to stick to our cover story in order to report on the genuine actions of people and see the real side of life on the streets.

At 11am sharp we advanced on Cardiff Central train station and saw the tell-tale sign of a TV interview; a man in a suit setting up a camera on a tripod. Carl was to be the presenter and cameraman this morning and he looked up to see two 'wandering whiffs' that surely needed no introduction. Trampface was about to hit the telly. We shook hands with Carl and he commented on how fresh we seemed considering our ordeal. He was lucky that we had our trainers on. The interview was fun and drew some inquisitive glances from nosy passers-by, clearly puzzled by the tramp-like celebrities. It was a fairly short affair which I put down to our professionalism in front of the camera and definitely not Carl's desire to escape the stink emanating from us. He told us the interview would air that evening at the end of the news, like a local feel good story to end on.

After a week of hardship and constant daily effort we were in line for a luxurious finale. We had started early on the Friday morning a week ago so we were now officially across the finishing line of Trampface Hitchhike with the full seven days completed. All that was left was to make our own way home as free men back in society. We'd anticipated paying for a train back to Swansea but our legend friend Lisa Brown gave us news that GWR were going to deliver us home VIP style. Sharon, the duty station manager, met us at the barrier and led us to the first class lounge which was otherwise closed on a Bank Holiday.

We spun some stories to Sharon and chatted whilst waiting for the train to arrive and enjoyed a bottle of water. Then we were escorted to the first-class carriage and handed over to Karl who would supply us with drinks and snacks the whole way home. Feeling wiped out but content, we sat back in the comfy seats and reflected on the highs and lows of another unbelievable Trampface adventure.

We'd seen and experienced so much on a truly unforgettable journey up and down the country. The constant struggles of the homeless and devastating situations some people exist in were accompanied by gestures of heart-warming generosity and kindness. Rudeness and ignorance were evident at times but mostly masked by the positive side of humanity. None more so than our friends and family following the mission and donating in droves. We had once again been humbled by all aspects of the adventure and learned even more about life in our country.

It was exhausting, mentally brutal at times, but an unbelievable voyage and totally unique. We had loved it. And I hope you enjoyed reading about it just as much. Paul jumped off the train at Port Talbot and as ever we enjoyed a warm, manly embrace, a handshake and the immortal words, "Joonooo, see ew soon my boy." I arrived at Swansea train station alone and paid scant attention to the line of taxis before slipping in my earphones to walk the couple of miles home. You can take the Tramp out of Trampface, but you can't do it that easily, or quickly.

Finally, back at home and after watching our scruffy faces on the ITV Wales news, it was time for a hot shower and a beer.

"Mission complete Tramp 1,"
"Mission complete, Tramp 2,"

HITCHHIKE REFLECTIONS

"The Forgotten Mission"

As this book goes to 'print' there have been five Trampface missions (oops, spoiler), with Hitchhike being the third in line. Despite this, whenever I get into a conversation with friends or family that have followed the missions they always think that there's only been four, with Hitchhike forgotten or overlooked. "Oh yeaaaa, the hitchhike one. I forgot about that," is a common reply. I guess it's a fair one; of all the missions, on the face of it, it does come across as the least remarkable or punchy. I personally think it has been very much underrated and hope you do too after reading it. Maybe we didn't push, or sell it enough at the time and I can see how it wasn't as ground breaking as the others. Trampface Swansea was our first venture into the unknown and Calais was just ridiculously dangerous and out of the box. The fourth one was insanely difficult to achieve and the fifth was completely and utterly insane and caused a national incident, ending in arrest; as you will find out. But I definitely think Hitchhike had its own character and presented its own unique challenges.

I felt a very different dynamic whilst writing it and really noticed how much easier it was to gain momentum and flow through the chapters. I also spent a lot of time laughing and having to immediately email Tramp 2 a couple of paragraphs that had me buzzing; Batman Bill and Mongolian Julian, for example. With Trampface Swansea and Calais I really had to concentrate and try hard to bring out the difficult issues of reality that we'd encountered. It was at times difficult and I'd put pressure on myself to make sure I was doing justice to the characters we'd met and the situations they were in. This caused me to avoid writing for long periods for fear of not being able to muster the quality of writing needed.

However, with Hitchhike, it wasn't just the writing that had a different and more relaxed feel to it; the mission itself took on a personality of its own. There was no doubt that we had witnessed the same hardship and heart-breaking situations on Hitchhike as on the previous two missions but the whole week seemed a lot more carefree, like we had set off from the start to just have as much fun as possible and really make the most of the characters we met. We still took the issues seriously but tried to make light of them at every opportunity. This is also how I felt writing it and I hope that has been reflected in your reading of it. This book took me just two months to write between Christmas, a full-time job in the Royal Marines and a month-long trip to the Arctic Circle, where the final word was struck. A fact that I find quite cool (yes literally) as the first book was edited and finished in the Arctic and the last few chapters and final words of Calais were completed in a tent in the Albanian mountains; whilst training the Kosovan security forces.

I finished writing Hitchhike on 14th February, St Valentine's Day. A quick look at my facebook page whilst in Northern Norway reminded me that it was of course the anniversary of the live radio proposal/stitch up of Tramp 2. What a great coincidence.

Maybe my mood and personal position, before and after, were factors in this slightly different approach and outlook. During the build-up I hadn't felt the same level of low mood and apprehension. It had been a positive build up and I was feeling good and relishing getting away. We always put ourselves under pressure, experiencing a little self-doubt as to whether we would encounter funny and interesting situations to put in the updates. That feeling was present again but I guess we had come to realise that funny people and incidents tend to land in our lap and we didn't really have much left to prove. We could just enjoy the week and have a laugh.

The immediate aftermath of the adventure was different also. After the first Trampface I'd felt extremely down and contemplative about what we'd been through and the people we'd left behind in the same position of desperation. I longed for the simple routine we'd had that week and even went out on the streets with a can of cider, hoping to bump into some of them. This time it was different, and I easily and happily slipped back into my life. Was this because I had dived straight into a trip away afterwards or that we had maybe become desensitised to life on the streets and the sights we had seen? Perhaps it was a mix of the two?

Hitchhike had been completed using our annual leave; for me it was my two weeks for Easter, so I still had a full week left. Time to rest up and recover at home? Nope. I had bought a brand-new Ford Custom van over Christmas with the view to converting it into a campervan in a fit suitable to my needs. Just prior to this year's adventure it had been completed. I named her 'Big Wednesday' in homage to a cult surf movie starring Gary Bussey and a classic '90s TV programme called '*Game On'*. I had planned a Lone Wolf tour of North Wales in Big Wednesday with my mountain bike. It would be a liberating week away from the norm but I would be joined by a friend for the first few days though.

My Brazilian friends Danni and Lucy (mentioned in chapter one) that I had met through couchsurfing had planned a trip to Wales. I'd probably got a little bit carried away and underestimated how tired I'd be; the girls were arriving on the afternoon that I finished Hitchhike. Danni rang me and told me that she and Lucy had fallen out so she was coming alone. I managed a quick hour of sleep on the sofa before driving down to pick her up. Sleep, do that when you're dead hey?

Danni is a really happy, lively, talkative, lovely girl so I knew it would be a good few days travelling up to North Wales. The first night she arrived was a Friday and we had arranged a night out with the view to set off in the morning. We hit the town in Swansea and had a few beers whilst being each other's wingmen, taking turns to approach members of the opposite sex to chat them up for each other for a laugh.

The next day we set off for Snowdonia and Danni said that her mother had told her that she must go and see West Wales. She made me laugh when I asked which part and she replied, "Umm just West Wales," as though it was a single location. After more probing and the same answer of, "West Wales," I explained that it is a region and has over ~~a~~ 100 miles of coast line. We settled on historic St David's, with its spectacular cathedral, and a couple of smaller coastal towns.

It was evening by the time we reached Llanberis, a village in the shadow of the peak of Snowdon, Wales' highest mountain. We had a couple of red wines and Danni settled into her B&B whilst I enjoyed my first night in Big Wednesday. The next day Danni wanted to climb Snowdon but the weather was atrocious and she didn't have all the correct gear for going on the mountain. I didn't feel comfortable negotiating the volatile and treacherous conditions up there unless fully prepared. We drove around the lakes and winding roads of Snowdonia instead and then visited the majestic castle at Caernarfon; where Prince Charles had his investiture. Our little trip ended with a pub crawl around the Roman walled city of Chester before Danni got the night train back to London.

Left on my own, I spent the remainder of the week touring the North Wales coast, finding spots to park up and then tear off on my bike. During one afternoon I was sat in a pub in Bangor, having a pint and writing for my book about my time in the Royal Marines. It was here I also witnessed some more of the sense of humour from the blind community. An elderly gentleman and his wife-had been sat at the table next to me and she had gone to the bar. I politely asked the gentleman if he would keep an eye on my laptop whilst I went to the toilet and he kindly agreed, with a wry smile. On my return his wife had re-joined him and as I sat down he spoke to her, "Trust a South Walian to ask the only blind man in the pub to look after his possessions while he went to the toilet. No wonder you lot lost everything to the Romans."

His wife laughed and I joined in with her. I then replied, "No wonder we don't trust you Gogs (Slang for North Walian) when you agree to watch something for us when incapable." We enjoyed a friendly chat and he told me the story about his condition,

"For decades I spent each day walking up to the summit of Snowdon. Up and down each day without fail. On this one day I returned and felt a strange headache and dizziness. I shook it off as a slight fever or something and went to sleep. I woke up the next morning blind. I opened my eyes but could see nothing but blankness. It was terrifying, it was torture and I was in a complete panic. How do you cope with the prospect of suddenly never being able to see the things you relied on each day? The realisation that such a basic and beautiful thing that you had taken for granted was now gone forever. You told me you are writing a book with your computer there? Please promise me you will keep reading, writing and encouraging people to do the same. It's such a gift and I miss it so much, I have gladly accepted my fate but very much wish to prompt more people to enjoy the pleasure of reading. To hear young ones get so excited about books makes me more happy than reading a book myself."

I was completely blown away by Richard and it transpired that he was also a writer, a published author, unlike the drunken wannabe that I was. Richard J. Bernard was not a native Welsh man; he was a Londoner who had moved to Wales as a child. He fell in love with the town of Beddgelert and the townsfolk with him. In 2013 he released his book '*A Snowdonia Childhood*', paying homage to his village and the upbringing it afforded him. I kept my promise to him to keep reading and writing and hopefully you will one day read this remarkable gentleman's book.

The remainder of my trip generally consisted of a couple of beers to relax at night, sometimes with a fire, and I felt extremely relaxed and content. It was a carefree but active week and I felt utterly invigorated at the end of it. There was one thing playing on my mind though, a task I had been putting off until the last minute in typical Westy fashion.

Tramp 2's wedding was less than a week away; I had been honoured to be chosen to be his best man. The problem? I hadn't even started on my speech…

TRAMPFACE: THE WEDDING

"Listeners, we need your help! Has anybody seen Paul and Westy, the Groom and Best man?"

I'd arrived home from my Lone Wolf excursion around North Wales the day before Tramp 2's stag do; a Saturday. Because of the short turn around, people's availability and cost, we had opted for a day go-karting and a night out in Cardiff. Not much time to work on my speech that weekend either; the other drama being that our friend Tomo was joint best man. This had repercussions for me wanting to do my usual routine of rushing it at the last minute and rolling with a bit of ad lib; Tomo and I would need a meeting to coordinate. The big day was set for the following Thursday and I was back on camp for my job instructing on a Royal Marine promotion course. "You could do it in the evenings on camp Westy," I hear you say… I could, apart from the fact that the first three days of the course would be spent on the bleak hills of Dartmoor. "You're an idiot Westy," I cursed to myself.

The stag do was great, plenty of carnage at the go-karting and a fair bit afterwards in a live music bar. We also had a quick pint in Wetherspoons to reminisce about being there in extremely different circumstances just a week earlier. It was going great until around 10pm when I noticed Tramp 2 had been missing for some time. I looked and asked around but to no avail and was now in danger of being accused of losing the Stag. A quick phone call to him established that he'd pulled one of his old tricks; he had slipped away unannounced and was on the train home. I won't repeat the names I called him before hanging up and continuing to enjoy the night.

My speech preparation was now left with no option other than to be written on my laptop on the freezing cold hills of Dartmoor. I had a good idea of the stories and things I wanted to say so just needed to write them down. I had also agreed with Tomo that he should just do his bit first then hand over to me. My word prep had been slacking but I had been proactive in some other areas…

You may remember on Day 5 during our lift to Leeds I smiled at the mention of Bear Grylls because I had been in secret contact with his team. Well, at the outset of our Hitchhike journey I had 'tweeted' Bear Grylls asking for a favour. He is an honorary Colonel in the Royal Marines from a bond that traces back to his father's service in the Corps. He does amazing work for the public presence of the Royal Marines and clearly has a fond affiliation with them. A little cheekily I had indulged in this connection to try and catch his attention. My tweet was: *Hi Royal (a common and respectful term used between Marines to address each other as brothers), I was wondering if I could ask a favour at all? If so could you send me a message on rmcommando@hotmail.co.uk?*

Paul had seen this public tweet and naturally assumed I was trying to get Bear to promote our current Trampface mission. When asked I agreed that that was the case, of course. But just like the interview on the radio station, I was bluffing him. I had received a reply from Bear's project manager in a matter of minutes after posting my request, which was surprising and very impressive for a team managing such a high profile and busy celebrity. The email read:

Hi there Lee, This is Lily from Bear Grylls Ventures. I understand you may have a message for Bear? Please do feel free to send it to me and I will be more than happy to pass it on.
Look forward to hearing from you
Lily

It's not often you get the ear of such a massive celebrity with the possibility of them fulfilling a request for a favour, so I laid it on thick with my email response:

Hi Lily, Wow I didn't expect such a prompt and friendly reply. My message to Bear is below, thank you for your reply and time.

Hi Mr Grylls, (my fellow Royal).

My name is Lee West and I am a serving Sergeant in the Royal Marines, I wonder if you could spare 2 minutes to help me please.
I am one half of a charity project duo called Trampface, each year we give up a week of our leave to go homeless, sleeping rough and begging with no support and a cover story. Online donations go to SSAFA the amazing military charity. This is our 3rd year and we are close to £10,000 for SSAFA. Last year we went undercover in the Calais 'Jungle'.

My oppo in this is Paul O'Dwyer who has just given me the honour of being his best man. The wedding is paid for by local radio from a competition they won. It's in April.
Paul is a massive fan of you and your achievements and actually led me to your book years ago. I wonder if there would be any chance you could record a small "Best wishes" video for me to use during my speech on the big day. Anything would help really, just a clip from a smart phone or anything.

We are both very aware of your affiliation with the Royal Marines and your fathers influence. Paul is not a Bootneck but has the highest regards and forever regrets never joining with me years ago... he actually got deployed to Iraq preventing him joining with me.

Any help would make his day and provide me loads of Best man brownie points!! I'm sorry to take your time as I imagine you are 'toppers' with work and messages and wish you all the best for the future.

We actually start this year's adventure tomorrow (March 18th). We are hitchhiking and sleeping rough. Below is evidence of our page and the Just Giving donation page. Feel free to have a read at our adventure updates and the live radio proposal.

Many Regards
Lee West

In less than a day from my email message I received another reply from Lily:

Hey Lee,
Hope this earns you some brownie points! Thanks for getting in touch and I hope the wedding goes swimmingly! And wishing you lots of luck for the new mission, keep up the fantastic work.
Best,
Lily.

The email had an attachment which was very exciting. I had opened the email quickly but couldn't risk keeping it open or clicking on the attachment while Paul was next to me. That night while he lay snoring next to me, signalling that the coast was clear I opened my phone and clicked on the attachment. I was over the moon with what I saw; Bear Grylls holding his smartphone in selfie mode and delivering a personalised message from the outdoors somewhere on set. His message was, "Hi Paul, Bear Grylls here. Wishing you all the best on your wedding day and hope you have a great time. We're thinking of you Royal."

Boom. I wriggled with excitement knowing that he was going to be absolutely stunned when we played this at his wedding. It was also made all the more special that I had received it during Hitchhike and watched it whilst he was sleeping next to me (on a pile of needles and human shit as it later turned out). I'd also got a video from the breakfast show hosts, Badger and Claire, and the Welsh singer Katherine Jenkins. I couldn't wait to see his and Ceri's faces when I played them, but that all depended on us actually making the ceremony of course…

"Another treble whisky please barman." Tomo, Paul's oldest friend from school and my co-best man was on a mission; not to get himself hammered but to inflict it on Tramp 2. We had met at a local bar across the road from Paul's house the night before the big day. "Food and a couple of quiet ones," it was sold as. Tomo was having none of it and was relentlessly putting drinks in front of him. I consider myself as one of the lads, always game for stitching each other up and high jinks but I wasn't comfortable with this. It was a big, busy day with lots of eyes and cameras on Paul and Ceri and considering it was arranged by radio and media we didn't want to make a fool of ourselves.

"Tomo, leave it out mate. He's going to be hammered, I want him to be fresh and enjoy tomorrow. Plus, you know he can't handle shorts," I pleaded.
"Fuck him, he did the same to me the night before my wedding so he's having it," was Tomo's stubborn retort.
"Well I wouldn't know mush as you didn't invite me to your wedding, remember," was my jab to bring up the past that had always made Tomo apologise to me. Even though I didn't mind I still liked playing on it.
"Ahhh come on mush, I said sorry for that. I explained why."
"Well leave Paul alone and I'll never mention it again," was my final bargaining chip. It didn't work, Tomo dismissed my words and carried on plying the Groom with Scotland's finest.

I told Paul to just leave the drinks but his pride and his mind set to not look weak in front of his mates led him to force the drinks down, one cringe after another. Closing time finally came and I was tasked with getting him to bed. I'd only had a couple of drinks so felt fine and managed to negotiate him across the road without incident. The two of us were staying in his house and Ceri was with her sister Beth. Paul was on the top floor of their townhouse with me a floor below. A good rest and we would be raring to go for the morning meet up…

Paul is a notoriously early riser. He suffers with bouts of insomnia but even so will rise at the crack of a sparrow's fart. I can barely recall many situations in our 20 years of friendship, be it a boy's weekend or hiking trip, that he hasn't been up and about before me. So, when I woke up at around 7am on the morning of the wedding I checked my phone and laid back to relax, safe in the knowledge that if he wasn't awake already he would soon be at my door saying, "Joonnoooo, alright my boy?" I sent him a quick text message about looking forward to the day and chilled out for a bit.

However, Tramp 2 wasn't awake or even close to it, he was unconscious in a deep, whisky induced sleep.

I'd drifted back off to sleep and without my safety alarm of Tramp 2 we were now in a perilous position without any awareness. During our extended slumber the Wave radio station had rung Ceri to get a friendly update on her preparations on air. They had then tried, and failed, to do the same with us; Paul's phone had gone straight to answer phone and mine had rung out. The presenters were ringing us live on air and at first people must have thought it was a prank. That was until after several attempts to contact us they reached out to others involved in the day who also said they hadn't heard from us. All whilst we lay in slumber totally oblivious to the manhunt being conducted.

"Listeners of Swansea and South Wales, we desperately need your help. The Groom and Best man for our 'Get me to the altar' wedding at Oldwalls today are missing. Their phones are off or not responding and they are running short on time to meet the wedding cars. They were last seen leaving the Bar Galois in Aberavon last night sometime after midnight. We need to find the Groom and Best man ASAP, has *anybody* seen Paul O'Dwyer or Lee West?"

I awoke with a big gasp of air and sat up to check my surroundings; I checked my watch and saw that it was gone 9 o'clock. We were meant to be at Paul's parents' house already dressed for the photographer to take some snaps and then jump in the cars. It was a fair drive of around an hour from Port Talbot to Oldwalls on the Gower Peninsula. I fell into a blind panic and couldn't fathom why Paul hadn't woken us. On legging it up the stairs to his room I found out why, he was still out for the count.

I shook Tramp 2 awake and told him the time; he immediately leapt up and turned his phone on. A collection of missed calls, voicemails and text messages came flooding through. The main protagonist was Claire from the Wave and Paul immediately rang her back. She was delighted to find we were alive and well and we enjoyed some banter with Paul saying, "It's Okay, we've just been doing some painting and decorating that's all. We were listening to Radio X though, sorry." It was actually quite funny and a good bit of drama for the radio that we had been genuinely missing in action for a couple of hours. We had quick showers and got our suits on ready for the big day.

The cars arrived and the Groom would be arriving in style; a brand new Range Rover Sport. Tramp 1 would not be cruising with him though; I would be driving Big Wednesday to the venue. Why? Because it is an exclusive wedding venue out of the way on the Gower Peninsular, my best man duties would require that I be the last man standing with the groom and therefore I would have to stay the night. Exclusive venue means exclusive price, which when weighed up with the option of my double bed campervan for free, had a clear winner. Plus, my fridge in Big Wednesday would be keeping my craft IPA beers nice and chilled for me to pop back and load my jacket up with every so often. Beats queuing to pay £5 at the bar!

Once a scrounging tramp, always a scrounging tramp!

The wedding went amazingly. Bride and Groom looked outstanding and the sun shone down on a fantastic day at a magnificent venue.

Tramp 2 did make me laugh when they were waiting on me for a photo whilst I was talking to some of the radio station girls. He called over, "Stop flirting with the girls and get over here." One of them replied, "He's not flirting, he's telling us about Trampface." To which Paul replied jovially, "That's his idea of flirting mun."

The time came for the speeches and it's fair to say we got our fair share of airtime. They were so epic that I made the decision to call the planner over and suggest that we have a half-time interval to allow people to refill glasses, smoke and pee. It always annoys me when people moan at weddings about speeches being quite long, for me they are the highlight of the reception party. I love having a drink and relaxing to listen to them and don't understand why people grumble; if you didn't have the speeches it would just be a meal, some drinks and a disco. You can do that anytime.

Anyway, the speeches got a little emotional with hugs getting dished out and the look on Paul's face when we played the Bear Grylls video was to treasure. I don't think he even watched it; he just stared at me with his mouth wide open. I declared that they were just a couple of words from my mates down the pub and then the party started in earnest.

Throughout the night a few questions were asked about Trampface Hitchhike and also, "What on earth are you going to do next year?" Well, we didn't want to let on quite yet, but we had indeed already started planning our next adventure… and boy was it going to be a cracker.

RUNNING ON EMPTY

"Marathon Madness"

Not long before the wedding day we did our last trawl for donations online, consolidated the begging money and our contributions and went firm on the final total for Trampface Hitchhike. We then posted it on the page for all to see the fantastic amount they had made possible; we also left a little lead into the next mission:

That's it, we've just paid in the begging cash/donation money and have the final total for Hitchhike. You are all legends for donating and SSAFA will continue to support our service families in hard times even more with your generosity. With all cash and Giftaid (I paid the £296 begging money in from my account and claimed £75 Giftaid... don't tell the taxman) we have a grand total of...

£3,101. Wow.
It's been a pleasure again this year and we are chuffed that you all enjoyed the updates. The wheels are in motion for Trampface Mk 4. Standby because it's a bit of a wildcard...
Loads of LOVE
Tramp 1 & Tramp 2. Xxxxxx

On return to work I found a package had been delivered to me at the Sergeants Mess. Not expecting anything I looked at the thin, brown, rectangle envelope in curiosity and read the front of it which was vaguely addressed to: Sergeant Lee 'Trampface', The Sergeants Mess, Commando Training Centre, Lympstone.

It was clearly from someone that had met me but only had minimal contact information. I opened it and discovered a very heart-warming, handwritten note inside:

Lee,

Many thanks indeed for the use of your AA insurance the other day. Without it the experience would have been much more painful, not to say much more expensive.

I hope your week on the streets of Cardiff was both successful and not too uncomfortable. In fact, your activities put me in mind of the enclosed book – perhaps you have already read it? Perhaps not.

Best wishes and renewed thanks,

Steve.

Wow, a very personal and touching gesture and letter indeed. The book was *George Orwell: Down and Out in Paris and London* and I had not in fact read it yet. It was of course from our first hitch out of Swansea, Steve the software engineer and former Royal Navy Officer. As Steve had mentioned during our ride, he had no social media/online presence at all so would not have read any of our updates and posted the book on the information remembered from our chat. The letter had no return address and at the top simply said: *Harrogate, 21 March.*

I was lifted by Steve's kind words and that he had truly appreciated meeting us, the feeling was mutual. It's unlikely we will ever see, or hear from, Steve again but if you ever do see this book, Cheers mate… hope you've now got a new car and AA cover!

We were keen to get the next Trampface mission laid down and had been floating some ideas around in the days immediately after Hitchhike. The main theme of our ideas was a wish to include some kind of physical challenge in with the homeless aspect. What better way to up the ante and difficulty levels than to impose physical hardship into the mix of little sleep and a poor, ad hoc diet. Cycling between towns, rowing across stretches of water and scaling the three peaks of the UK were all mooted. We were in and around the area of nailing something down when the talk turned to transitioning straight into an organised distance cycling or running event. Finish the week with testing ourselves whilst in a state of physical and mental degradation.

A meeting was scheduled at Trampface HQ AKA the Wetherspoons pub, Swansea. Prior to the meeting Tramp 2 had been asking me for my details such as DOB, full address etc. The reason why would soon reveal itself after a few pints of American IPA. The mission was three quarters agreed on; we would start in Swansea and cycle around 50 miles a day to another city, lock up our bikes and become homeless for the rest of the day and night following the same rules as normal. We just needed an end state and little did I know, we had already been entered into one…

Paul revealed what he had been up to, “We cycle and live rough for five nights, making our way towards London via some key towns and cities. Once we arrive in the capital we go homeless there for two nights, which will be tough and a real eye opener. Then on the final morning after seven days cycling 50 miles a day and seven nights sleeping rough, with a shocking diet we will crawl out from a bush and run the London Marathon.”

I nearly sprayed my pint all over Tramp 2. The idea was bonkers, completely and utterly bonkers. I loved it. It was surely one of the worst ways to prepare for a full-length marathon but what a challenge it would be. London is also one of the most prestigious marathons in the world so the occasion would be exhilarating. Paul saw me smiling and said, “What do you think my boy?”

“It’s a ridiculous idea… but I’m one hundred percent keen my boy.”

Paul gave me a knowing smile of mischief, sipped his pint and then said, “Well, that’s a relief to know my boy… because I’ve already signed us up.”

EPILOGUE

"A Bump in the Road"

This book was started and finished in under three months, utilising the archived daily updates from Tramp 1 and 2. With it being my third book I had my routine of getting it published pretty squared away; proof, send to friend and colleague Rebecca to proof, get cover artwork done, upload, release. The final word was struck in February whilst in the Arctic Circle, however, come June I was still trying to complete the process when a turn of events led to a serious delay in the release of Trampface Hitchhike.

I had been serving in Portsmouth as a Colour Sergeant and the Chief Instructor of the Royal Marines Band new entry recruits. No, I wasn't some instrumental wizard, I was charged with bringing these wannabe musicians up to a soldiering standard in order to serve under the title of 'Royal Marine'. Once my team had finished with them they would progress and undergo their intense military band training, graduating as proficient in two instruments as a minimum.

During June word was put out that a celebrity, earlier mentioned in this book was paying a visit to us. Bear Grylls' son Marmaduke had expressed an interest in joining the Royal Marines band one day and his high profile Dad, an honouorary Colonel, had arranged the trip. I spoke to the Officer Commanding and expressed a desire to meet Bear and present him with a copy of my second book. He had sent me an acknowledgement of receiving my first book which I'd sent as a thank you for recording a video of well wishes to Tramp 2. I'd used it on a big screen during my bestman's speech at Tramp 2's wedding. My wish to be present was granted.

I awaited eagerly at the entrance to our enclosure (a former Victorian era prison, with the recruits each allocated a 'cell' to practice in) with a signed copy of Trampface: Calais in my combat trouser pocket. Bear arrived in uniform complete with the Royal Marines Green Beret. He was met by the senior musician officers whom I had a great amount of respect for and enjoyed a seamless working relationship with. Almost immediately he focused on me as the only other rank there sporting the coveted Commando Green Beret and made a beeline to ask what my role was at the school of music.

He was led around the school and observed various displays from the recruits playing their instruments to the precision of military coordination in tune and movement. He regularly gave genuine praise for the abilities and dedication of the band and touched on the morale and support they provide to the wider Royal Marines family. The time came for the obligatory photo opportunity and I waited on the fringe whilst the musicians lined up for snaps. To my surprise, Bear called over for me to join him for a photo and I eagerly accepted, knowing it would be a perfect time to also present him a copy of my second book.

I gave a little introduction before handing over the copy and once again to my surprise he responded by saying, "Thank you Colours, that's great. I really enjoyed your first book." Wow, I thought to myself, Bear Grylls has actually read about Tramp 1 and 2. He may have just been saying it to be polite of course but the fact he'd remembered my book without mention of it by me was still impressive. The encounter was about to get even better.

Huw, the Band Major prompted me to tell Bear about the most recent Trampface mission which had led to our arrest and detention by a host of UK security forces, including Border Force and some high level detectives. This had all happened prior to arrival at my new post in Portsmouth so my introduction when I arrived and explained the ongoing saga to Huw and the team was interesting to say the least. The above mentioned recent mission was the fifth installment of our Trampface insanity and I still have to write book four first so do not want to go into too much detail at this point!

I gave Bear a quick rundown of the recent challenge which had culminated in an attempt to cross the English Channel from Northern France to Kent… or anywhere on UK soil. It was planned to assess the difficulties and/or ease of migrants using this route to slip into the UK; a very topical story in the media at the time. I

explained that this was attempted in a nine foot dinghy, at night, in a force 9 wind, across the busiest shipping lane in the world… after 7 nights living homeless, of course. Bear seemed gripped by the story of adventure and considering his own endeavors in life and on TV was quite the compliment, but he saved his best reaction until my reply to his final question, "That's pretty edgy stuff, what kind of support team and safety system did you have in place? How many boat crews were there shadowing you?
I looked him in the eye and said, "None, there was no other boat or person there apart from us, and no-one knew where we were once we had set off into the inky black night. We saw a red mast light which we assessed was the English coast and off we went into the surf unsupported."

Bear Grylls, the 'Man vs Wild', the youngest man to climb Everest after recovering from a broken back and numerous daring escapades now took a step back with his jaw dropped. He scrutinised me for a moment and realising I was serious exclaimed, "Unsupported? That is absolutely insane!"

We chatted a little more and we posed for a photo with a copy of Trampface, which he later posted on his facebook and twitter accounts giving praise to Trampface and mentioning that it was a pleasure to see Colour Sergeant Lee West. His twitter alone had 1.2m followers, amazing. As enjoyable and rewarding as this encounter was, it was to have far more negative consequences for the release of the third Trampface book. This would be due to the utterly ignorant, idiotic, childish, short sighted and authoritarian nature of certain officers in the Royal Navy Command and media communications departments.

My problems arose from the previously mentioned mission attempting to cross the English Channel in a dinghy. For obvious reasons we had kept the finale to our fifth Trampface mission secret from our daily blogs and anyone apart from close friends and family who rightly needed to know. I'd also informed my immediate superiors in work who had all been aware of my Trampface background and books. We weren't doing anything illegal like smuggling actual migrants (you'll have to read book five for the hilarious revelation of who/what we did have in the boat) so it wasn't an issue, it was an extracurricular activity during my time on leave; some people row the Atlantic or cycle to John O'Groats… we try to kill ourselves in a dinghy!

The aftermath of our audacious maritime challenge was too much to cover here but in short, the Navy had burst into the office of the Commandant General of the Royal Marines exclaiming that one of his men had been smuggling immigrants across the channel, untrue of course… sort of (read book 5!). The end result being that I was on their radar and no doubt they were annoyed at dealing with this on a weekend during Easter leave. Fast forward to Bear Grylls posting on social media about me and my books from which they decided to go on a witch hunt and trawl my social media. Here they found a post from me a few weeks earlier proudly stating that my third book was written, edited and waiting on artwork to release. Pretty benign and not in violation of anything you'll find; not to the conclusion jumping ranks of the Royal Navy Media it wasn't.

I can only imagine what buffoonery went on when they saw this tweet and became so hell bent in taking action against me that it blinded them to the fact that this book had absolutely nothing to do with the latest dinghy episode and had been conducted three years prior. The tweet even explained exactly what the book was about, hitchhiking homeless around the UK; it was pretty plain to see. Why would a little fact that it was years ago and had no connection to the recent event get in their way though? I've no doubt that a factor in this pursuit of me was to do with control. The fact that I had released books and had Bear Grylls, an honourary Royal Marine who they no doubt swoon over for the amazing free publicity he gifts them, promoting me online. All without their 'Big Brother' style blessing of approval.

I was summoned to appear in front of the Commanding Officer (CO) and explain why he had received an email from the media department asking him to speak to me. I had nothing to hide and explained all about Trampface and the fact that the Navy had got their wires crossed, again. I expressed my dismay that they had not approached me in person to discuss this and had adopted a position akin to a school prefect telling tales. The CO was a calm and levelheaded officer and agreed that there seemed to be no malice or wrong doing from me but was duty bound to report back and await their instructions. The next day I was ordered to send the full manuscript of this book to the CO to forward to the media team. Once again they remained faceless and nameless using the CO as a go-between. Whilst I waited for more developments I was presented with a letter from Navy Command which laid bare their utter ignorance to this whole affair and exposed it for the charade that it was. When you read the below snippet, just bear in mind their comments about crossing the channel and the government stance on the migrant situation; things that have nothing to do with the book that my tweet clearly explained.

I was raging at this arrogant and condescending attitude towards me and my Trampface project. I felt like I was being considered as some sort of rogue who needed to be reined in. The bottomline of their verdict was that any 'communication on contentious or non-contentious subjects must be cleared', so basically anything them. What kind of dictatorship did I belong to where you literally couldn't say anything outside of the forces without asking pretty please to some jumped up officer. I found it utterly pathetic and archaic.

A part of me was hell bent on refusing them access to a copy of my book, which I'm sure legally I could have. I also had the desire to say, "Screw them" and release the book anyway. After some contemplation I decided to play the long game, as frustrating as it was after working so passionately on the book during my spare time. I had a medical board assessment on the horizon and was looking at a likely medical discharge due to my loss of hearing. If and when that decision was made I would then be free to release my book and of course include this chapter saying what I thought about the whole distasteful treatment towards me. I sent the manuscript and left a parting shot in my email which would no doubt irk a few upturned noses at Navy Command. I signed off with:

I would like to advise you that the content and material attached to this email, Trampface Hitchhike, remains the intellectual property of L.G. West and any unauthorized reproduction, distribution or use of it is in breach of copyright.

A month and a half later I had still not received any guidance or correspondence regarding my book. Summer leave was around the corner and I made a request for information. My three weeks leave could be spent preparing the book for release but instead I received no clear direction and my plans were left in limbo. In the meantime Tramp 2 and I had bought a craft beer café bar in Swansea and attention turned to preparing our new adventure, Copper Bar, for its grand opening.

On my return from summer leave I requested a meeting with the new CO and asked if the matter could be chased up. I sat and witnessed a very confusing phonecall where Navy Command cited what they believed to be 'potential issues' with my book but refused to take responsibility for gagging me. The very people who had started all this now gave their two pence worth and sloped shoulders by saying, "The final call is on the Royal Marines HQ, who if sanction the release hold the responsibility of any negative outcome." That read to me in layman's terms as, "We've advised you to stop it but we are a bunch of shithouses too scared to take the decision ourselves and if we decide it's caused bad PR we will hang you and Colour Sergeant West out to dry."

I naturally enquired on what these potential issues from the book were, because I had still not received any direct contact from these ever so professional people interfering with my personal goals and achievements. The apparently controversial reasons that were going to sully the name of the Royal Navy/Marines were listed as such:

"You jumped a train without paying." My reply, "The transport police escorted us to the exit and told us to have a good night."
"You urinated in a public place." My reply, "We do that every time we go on a field exercise on Woodbury Common, a public place."

"You were in breach of tax rules by taking money from begging." My reply, "It was for charity, we could've claimed 25% gift aid tax relief on it."

So, these were the highly contentious issues I'd been run through the mill for and still nothing to do with their original beef about crossing the channel and the migrant situation. If you have read this and find that you feel I may have been a little harsh with my opinion then let me leave you with this… I received no apology for their blatant misinterpretation of my intentions, I was treated like some wayward scrotbag instead of the seventeen year senior marine that I was, I was gagged by an office of cowards who couldn't even muster the moral fibre to confront me themselves, I lost a year of momentum unable to release my work and finally I was left humiliated when I explained my counter points to their reasons above and was abruptly told, "Stop talking and listen," before being dismissed with the order not to release Trampface Hitchhike. The whole thing had left me deflated, disgruntled and for the first time questioning if Trampface was really worth it.

Only a group of shortsighted morons could assess the Trampface missions, fundraising and awareness as bad PR, in my opinion. But as it turns out 'bad press' was what they were panicking about and that is exactly what Trampface has now given them, just not in the way they predicted!

With my amazing and forever memorable time serving as an elite Royal Marines Commando over, I finally got to finish and release this book. The trilogy complete. The story does not end here though and you better get ready to limber up for what's to come. First up a couple of tramps at an international sporting event… and then a quite unfortunate but hilariously dangerous international incident; one which may well call time on the Trampface saga.

****

Thank you for reading Trampface Hitchhike. If you enjoyed following our adventure and would like news on any upcoming events or releases, then please feel free to contact me at Trampface@mail.com **I'd also love to hear any feedback, questions or opinions about my work. Currently there have been two more Trampface missions since this one so keep your eyes peeled for their release.**

You can also read some of my short stories detailing true accounts of an Afghan helicopter assault, Police raid and lone travel tales on my website: https://trampface.com/

If you have a couple of spare moments, I'd like to do some more Trampface begging and ask you to kindly leave me a review on Amazon. It really does make a massive contribution to the visibility of Trampface.

Trampface is now a part of the charity that we founded called SA1UTE. Our mission is to help people suffering with mental health and we have purchased a plot of woodland in Brecon to allow sufferers to get away and engage in activities. Or simply to relax in the tranquil environment. Type SA1UTE into any search engine and you can find us online.

Facebook: L.G. West – Author
Twitter: @Royal_Marine_LW
Instagram: westy_trampface

See you soon for Trampface Marathon.
Lots of Love

Tramp 1.